*Ellie*

"*The Butterfly Garden* is a work of art that transcends any memoir that I have ever read. This is a work that, once read, will never be forgotten."

—**Marc Klaas,** child advocate and founder,
KlaasKids Foundation

"*The Butterfly Garden* is a story of pain and despair, but more importantly, of astonishing courage and resiliency. It is a memoir, but also a mystery and a thriller, as Chip St. Clair tells of his tortured childhood at the hands of a sadistic father, a father with a dark and dangerous secret. *The Butterfly Garden* speaks to age-old themes of tragedy and triumph. But in the end, it is about the healing powers of hope and forgiveness. It is not to be missed."

—*Detroit Free Press*

"Chip St. Clair sets free a timeless work that will inspire. It's the only way to see what's really in a survivor's heart."

—**Mark Lunsford,**
The Jessica Marie Lunsford Foundation

"From a childhood of abuse at the hands of an angry and violent father, Chip St. Clair discovered an inner world to cope and survive. Even though he lived at the edge of darkness and despair, Chip's story of survival will inspire and give hope to many victims of child abuse."

—**United States Congressman Joe Knollenberg,**
Michigan

"Incredibly powerful. This will be an important book for years to come. If you don't understand the damage done to millions of American children by emotional and physical abuse, you need to read this book. If you understand it from firsthand experience, you especially need to read it, because Chip St. Clair's message about protecting others could change your life and the world."

—**Grier Weeks,** Executive Director, PROTECT,
The National Association to Protect Children

D0964360

"*The Butterfly Garden* is a book that inspires the soul when we are surrounded by darkness."

"*The Butterfly Garden* is the gripping tale of growing up with a child murderer, yet, at the same time, it is the story of an adult-survivor's personal search for justice. Chip St. Clair demonstrates that it is not only possible to evolve beyond one's dark past, but how the experience can fuel a crusade to make the world safer for others."

"Chip St. Clair brilliantly exemplifies the courage that remains in a child who has had his entire world destroyed on a regular basis by a perverse father —the same courage that remains as an adult when he decides not only to confront his enslavement, but to bare his soul in this book. His courage makes him a hero, his prose makes him an artist. Chip St. Clair can write. Were it up to me *The Butterfly Garden* would be required reading in middle schools; perhaps fostering the chutzpah of young people willing to stand up and name their accusers. And demand society's retribution."

"Truly inspiring. *The Butterfly Garden* motivates and gives the reader strength from the heart and spirit, leaving the thought, 'If Chip can survive and thrive, so can I.' A book everyone should read."

"Truly a great book! *The Butterfly Garden* is a riveting personal account of a child whose youth was tortured by a father's cruel and abusive nature who one day rose above the torment. Chip St. Clair is an inspiration to me and others he has impacted over the years—for the sake of every child in a similar plight I hope he keeps the message alive and keeps spreading his wings."

# The Butterfly Garden

A MEMOIR

## Chip St. Clair

**Health Communications, Inc.**
**Deerfield Beach, Florida**

*www.hcibooks.com*

To protect the identity of certain individuals, some of the names have been changed.

**Library of Congress Cataloging-in-Publication Data**

St. Clair, Chip.
  The butterfly garden / Chip St. Clair.
    p. cm.
   ISBN-13: 978-0-7573-0695-2 (trade paper)
   ISBN-10: 0-7573-0695-0 (trade paper)
   1. St. Clair, Chip. 2. Adult child abuse victims—United States—
Case studies. 3. Identity (Psychology)—United States—Case
studies. 4. Family violence—United States—Case studies. 5. Abusive
parents—United States—Case studies. 6. Criminals—United States—
Case studies. I. Title.
HV6626.52.S73 2007
362.76'4092—dc22
[B]

2007041647

© 2007 Chip St. Clair

HCI, its logos, and marks are trademarks of Health Communications, Inc.

Publisher: Health Communications, Inc.
    3201 S.W. 15th Street
    Deerfield Beach, FL 33442-8190

*Cover design by Larissa Hise Henoch*
*Interior design and formatting by Lawna Patterson Oldfield*

*This book is dedicated to
my friend, my love, my wife, Lisa—
a butterfly from the moment
I laid my eyes upon her.*

# CONTENTS

# ACKNOWLEDGMENTS

FIRST AND FOREMOST, my heartfelt gratitude to one of the strongest men I know, my father-in-law, Richard, and the memory of his wonderful wife, Karen.

For your passion and belief in this project from the beginning: Peter Rubie, Allison Janse, and the entire HCI family.

For your leadership, commitment, and dedication to fighting the good fight: John Walsh, Mark Lunsford, Marc Klaas, Alison Arngrim, Congressman Joe Knollenberg, Senator Mike Bishop, Prosecutor Dave Gorcyca, Sheriff Michael Bouchard, Representative David Law, Representative John Sinrud, and Randy Burton.

For all who believed in me, supported me, and inspired me . . . all of my many good friends and those I consider family—you know who you are.

And last but not least . . . William Ernest Henley.

# PROLOGUE

*The unexamined life is not
worth living for man.*

—Plato (469–339 BC)
Attributed to the character Socrates
in Plato's *Apology* dialogue

THERE IS FOR ALL of us a profound moment of truth that lies in wait—a moment that transfixes our attention and forces us to confront the essential questions in life: Who am I? What is my purpose?

For some, this moment is a blip on the radar soon ignored, a wayward stroke of insight never again considered. Yet for others it sparks enlightenment, a process of personal evolution through introspection. My moment of truth came in the form of a large, black trunk with a brass latch, when I was twenty-two. I remember the day I found it in my parents' home, secreted away in a place forbidden to me as a child. My own Pandora's Box.

That day, my fiancée Lisa and I tentatively entered my parents' apartment, and although no one was home—nor ever would be again—my heart raced with anxiety. I was looking for something, but I wasn't sure what.

We traced our way through rooms I had been in hundreds of times, searching through drawers and closets, finding nothing. We eventually made our way to the staircase. As we ascended, my legs became heavy, my steps slow and deliberate. If anything was to be found it would be in the room at the top of the stairs—their bedroom. Reaching the upper landing, I grasped the handle of the door before I could lose my nerve. With a quick glance at Lisa, I turned the knob and walked in.

The air was stale and musty. Dark shapes and shadows filled the room, for the heavy curtains drawn at the back blotted out all light save that which spilled in through the doorway. Placed neatly at the foot of my parents' bed was a trunk. It was not hidden. There was no lock, nor was there need for one. My father had ruled by fear, and fear can be more powerful than any lock. I trembled as I stood staring at the trunk. I felt very small. Years of being told never to ask questions about my past made me reluctant to approach, yet I forced myself to kneel before it. The seconds seemed like hours, as my hand rested on its latch. An unnerving quiet hung in the air—the stillness before a storm.

I might have seen the trunk a couple of times over the years— it's hard to recall. But I would never have dared to open it for fear of my father's wrath. I had no concern for him now. After twenty-six years on the run, he had been sent back to prison for murdering a three-year-old child almost thirty years earlier.

When my father's true identity was revealed to me I somehow lost my own. Everything I believed about my life had been a lie, and I began to search desperately for answers. I had spent all of my twenty-two years with my parents on the run; always moving, never knowing.

I undid the brass latch and raised the lid of the trunk. Inside, I found not answers but more questions. In silent horror I rummaged through forged birth certificates, pictures of other children with my name on them, falsified school records, locks of hair, and baby teeth—clues that alluded to an even greater mystery. The discovery left me reeling with doubt, confusion, and a gaping emptiness. I had opened the trunk yearning for answers about who I was. Instead I found that I couldn't even be sure of my own name or birthday. I didn't even know if the people I had called "Mom" and "Dad" were my real parents. Had I been kidnapped? Had there been other children in their care—children who had not survived my father's brutality?

In a very literal sense, this was my moment of truth—the beginning of my quest for my true identity. In a single moment I had been presented a unique opportunity to face the question we all must ask ourselves: Who am I?

Those who look within and find the answers they seek emerge transformed, with a renewed sense of focus, peace, and freedom—a freedom that flies beyond confusion, anger, and doubt—a freedom that flies to new heights of understanding, of hope. As my journey unfolded, I realized that I didn't simply wish to fly. I wanted to soar. . . .

# CHAPTER
## 1

# The Truth Shall
# Set You Free

I NEVER THOUGHT I would see a prison in real life, much less visit one. Oliver Wendell Holmes once wrote, "Sin has many tools, but a lie is the handle which fits them all."

"You're here for offender #37670," the guard confirmed, leading us down a narrow, dimly lit hallway.

"Yeah," I whispered, my voice echoing loudly in the cramped corridor.

"That's a real old number," he remarked. "You don't see too many that old. He sure has been gone a long time. All those years and you didn't even know?"

"No," I stammered, watching him turn a corner ahead. "It was only about a year ago when I found out . . . who he really was. What he had done. That's why I turned him in."

I glanced back at my fiancée Lisa and her father, grateful for their support. I was preparing to confront my father for the first time in my life to hold him accountable for all he had done to me. He had paralyzed me with fear, intimidation, and ridicule. He had tried to break me, day after day, year after year, imprisoning me with lies and deceit.

"Well, good luck," the guard said. Then he tipped his hat and motioned us into the large room where I would testify before the parole board.

Lisa reached out and squeezed my hand. Her father, Richard, grasped my shoulder warmly.

"You'll do fine," he assured me.

As I took a seat, I flipped through my black leather attaché case, trying to better organize my thoughts in anticipation of my testimony. There were miscellaneous documents, pictures of children, police reports, military records—all riddled with lies. I paused when I came across a small, pale-green sheet of paper, a birth certificate issued by the state of Indiana. I held it up toward the fluorescent light glaring above me, to be sure that the parole board could see through this particular lie. There it was, *Chip Anthony St. Clair*—along with all the other information on the sheet—typed over, forged. Even the birth date, *August 1, 1975*, was a lie.

I sighed and fished out the one piece of truth within the attaché case—a small, thin, blue book of poetry called *One Hundred and One Famous Poems*. This book represented my hope as a child, tucked away deep inside me. The comfort of its words had rescued me on more than one occasion, and I was going to call upon them today to rescue me once again.

The three of us sat quietly in the room until the parole board members finally filed in. Each of them carried a folder and wore an unreadable expression. I listened intently as they talked amongst themselves, trying to draw some conclusion as to what they were thinking and what they might think of me.

"So, this is his *son* that is going to speak?" one member asked.

"Well, that's not certain, but he grew up with him all those years," another whispered.

"Wasn't he convicted of second-degree murder . . . 1973?" mumbled a third.

"Yes, voluntary manslaughter," said a gray-haired man, glancing up at me.

They abruptly silenced themselves and took their places behind the desk. A gold nameplate identified each member. After clearing his throat, the head of the parole board called my name.

I rose from my chair and stepped toward the small table positioned before them. Steadying a shaky hand on the back of the chair, I pulled it out and sat down.

"Whenever you're ready," boomed the voice ahead of me.

With seven intense pairs of eyes watching me, I began to speak.

"My name is Chip St. Clair. I want to tell you about my life with Michael Grant . . ."

# CHAPTER
# 2

# Riding Out the Storm

I DIDN'T KNOW IF she would get up. She had stopped crying, and all I could hear was the dull sound of his foot connecting somewhere with her body. I was too afraid to watch anymore, which was what usually happened when the beating went on for more than five minutes. This time I stayed crouched behind the reclining chair, just out of his line of vision. I could still see the doorway to the kitchen.

"You goddamn bitch!" he bellowed in a voice that was hoarse from yelling.

I raised my hands to my ears, partly to muffle the sound of his voice, but also to deaden the sound of the blood pounding in my head. I held my breath and strained to hear her again. Nothing. *When would he stop?* I couldn't remember if I even jumped up in protest or tried to divert his attention to protect her. All I knew was that I was afraid, and this was one of my hiding places when it started.

I peered around the side of the chair and took note of my other hiding places. In the center of the living room was the wooden coffee table that matched the end tables. Everything in our apartment matched. My father liked it that way. He needed it that way or my mother ended up getting hurt. So he always got his way. But like tonight, the beatings still came. I wondered if it had something to do with dinner. Maybe it was overcooked or undercooked. Maybe the gravy was too runny. It was hard to know.

I couldn't remember when the abuse began, nor could I remember life without it. It seemed as if I was all of a sudden *there*, like going to sleep and being dropped right in the middle of a nightmare. You never analyze how you got there; you just try to make it through. That's what I did every day; I just tried to survive.

The coffee table used to be a good hiding place, with cupboards on both sides to store magazines and books. I used to be small enough to fit inside, but not anymore. Now that I was five years old, my legs had grown too long for me to fit into such a cramped space.

The floral-printed sofa to the left of the coffee table worked well, too. With bright red and yellow flowers, it seemed out of place in the room; it was too cheerful and didn't match anything else. Perhaps that was what the fight was about. I thought about moving to hide under the sofa because it had a skirt that swung down to meet the carpeting. I could hide there for hours without being noticed, but I didn't have enough time to make it there.

As soon as he had jumped up to grab her, I had dropped my fork and run from the table. Once out of the kitchen I had assumed my spot behind his La-Z-Boy, smelling the cigarette smoke that permeated the fabric. On the end table bordering the chair sat his ashtray filled with cigarette butts. He liked to smoke while he watched television. Those were the two things he did: smoke and watch television. His glass of Tab sat next to the ashtray. The ice cubes had melted, diluting the cola to an opaque, tea-brown color—one of his pet peeves. I prayed that he wouldn't notice.

Suddenly, his footsteps became louder as he stomped toward the entryway. I closed my eyes, hoping to somehow magically turn invisible or to wake up from this nightmare. I couldn't help but peek, though; I had to know where he was going.

As I slowly craned my neck around the chair, my eyes met his. When he spotted me, I stood up to face him, leaving my safe place. His swollen face was flushed red with anger. He wore a grimacing scowl laced with spittle, not unlike a rabid animal. But what I'll never forget were his eyes: The whites were a deep pink color and widened in a terrifying expression. He immediately closed the distance between us. His enormous girth loomed over me, and his thick fingers were clenched in fists at his sides.

"What the hell are you looking at, you little fuck?" he screamed, jabbing a finger inches from my face.

I opened my mouth to speak, but nothing came out. I felt my

heart pounding in my throat as tears traced their way back down my face. This enraged him even further.

"Don't you *dare* cry!" he ordered.

Wiping my eyes, I whispered, "I won't."

And then out of nowhere, he turned around and walked upstairs.

"You're all a bunch of cocksuckers!" He slammed the bedroom door so hard the apartment shook.

I let out the breath I had been holding as the tears returned. Slowly I crept toward the doorway to the kitchen, afraid of what lay beyond. I stopped just before I reached it and listened. Everything was silent. Trying my best to be brave, I peered into the kitchen. On the floor, among a collage of broken plates and spilled food, my mother lay seemingly lifeless, crouched in a fetal position with her hands curled into her stomach. Her face was already swollen from the slaps and punches. Her right eye was bruised and bleeding, her lips puffy. Blood was pooling on the floor.

"Mama?" I whimpered.

No response.

"Mama?" I tried again.

She took in a haggard breath and spoke with great effort. "Get away," she sobbed. "Leave me alone!"

And so she laid, her body racking with sobs as I began to cry harder. She didn't want me near her, but I couldn't leave. So I just stood there, watching her. The storm seemed to subside as quickly as it had begun. I had made it through another night.

# CHAPTER
# 3

# Unconquerable Soul

In the summer of 1983, I found myself in the backseat of my parents' gray Oldsmobile sedan, heading to northern Michigan for a weekend getaway. I welcomed the retreat into nature's embrace and the chance to see one of the Great Lakes, Lake Michigan, yet it would be years before I realized the significance of this trip.

The crunching of gravel under the tires told me we were very close. We had turned off the interstate and were heading down a long, winding back road. Large pines and other unfamiliar trees loomed overhead as we made our way through the dense forest.

"It's around here somewhere," my father said as he craned his neck, looking from side to side.

The car slowed and then rolled to a stop. "What the hell? They said in a quarter of a mile we would see another road to turn onto."

"I thought I saw a road a little ways back," my mother admitted meekly.

"Why the hell didn't you say so?"

"I didn't want to be wrong and have you get mad and scream at me."

"I wouldn't get mad and scream," he screamed. "Tell me where the goddamn thing is!"

Throwing the car into reverse, he stomped on the gas pedal, thrusting me into the back of my mother's seat. A few seconds later, she pointed. "There. Right there."

"That?" he asked. "You'd have to be Davy goddamn Crockett to find your way through there. What do you think we're driving—a bicycle? There's no room!"

Leaning over, I studied the path. It did seem awfully narrow, but it had obviously been well traveled.

"I see tire tracks," I said. "We can probably make it."

"Shut up," he barked.

He backed up a bit farther, put the car into drive, and then slowly crept onto the darkened path.

"We better not get one scratch on this car," he warned. "And this better be the right way."

"Do you want me to get in front of the car and guide you?" she offered.

"Yeah, get out there so I can run your dumb ass over. You shut up, too."

We soon came to a clearing. Cars were parked along the

pines bordering an open area, and a huge log cabin with smaller matching units was straight ahead.

"That must be where we check in," he said, pointing to the cabin.

A man in a blue shirt with a nametag over his pocket rapped a knuckle on the driver's window. "You come up for the weekend?" he asked, smiling.

"Yeah, Jerry," my father snapped, as he read the man's nametag. "Is this where we check in?"

"Uh-huh. This is the lodge, but you can't park here. This here's a fire lane."

"Is there a fire?" my father asked Jerry very seriously.

"Well . . . no. But . . ."

"Good." He pushed Jerry aside as he opened the door. "I'll only be a minute."

My mother stretched out her hand and held it poised above the door handle, watching my father approach the building. The moment he vanished inside, she threw open the car door.

"I'm gonna check if there are any scratches on the car," she said hurriedly.

Breathing a sigh of relief, she got back in just before my father came out of the lodge.

"The guy inside said we can rent a rowboat down at the dock," he grunted, the car rocking as he plopped back into the driver's seat. "Tomorrow morning we're going to row all the way across Lake Michigan to the other side!"

Another narrow road to the left of the lodge led to our cabin.

As we began unloading our luggage, I stole a glance at the building where we would be staying. The log-cabin style was similar to that of the main building, but smaller and more personal. As we entered, I noticed a warm, woodsy smell, like the forest itself but more intense. Drab furniture and mundane artwork adorned the interior, centered on a huge stone fireplace. A staircase across from the main living area led up to two bedrooms.

I placed my backpack on the bed in the smaller room and peered out the window. Beyond the expanse of trees was a great, shimmering body of water, a small inlet giving way to what appeared to be a vast sea. Waves rolling in the wind caught the sunlight, bouncing radiance back at the world. Lake Michigan. It seemed like an ocean to an eight-year-old. I strained to see the other side, but saw no land other than what stretched along our side of the lake.

"Chip," my father called from the master bedroom, "I'm gonna take a shower. You wanna take one, too?"

"No, I just wanted to look out the window. Maybe I'll unpack," I replied, walking over to the bed and sitting down.

While I unzipped my backpack, I heard footsteps coming from the other room. My father leaned his head through the doorway.

"Mom's downstairs making something to eat. You sure?" he asked wolfishly, his eyes growing wide. He threw his naked body into the room and danced toward me with his arms outstretched. I tried to pull away, but he stood beside me and pressed his genitals against my face.

"Whoo-hoo," he laughed.

"Dad, don't. That's gross," I objected, trying to force out a laugh.

"Okay," he said as he walked toward the door, "but I'll be in here if you need me." Turning around, he raised his eyebrows and smiled.

Once I heard the shower start, I ran downstairs to the other bathroom. Passing the kitchen, I heard the clinking of plates and glasses as my mother set the table. Confident that she hadn't noticed me, I darted into the small bathroom and locked the door. The room contained only a sink and a toilet, and barely enough space for one person. I turned on the faucet and waited for the water to get warm while I unwrapped the small bar of soap that had been neatly placed on the wooden counter. I lathered my hands and scrubbed vigorously, washing the sickening memory of his warmth and sweat from my face.

I always washed my face after he did that. *Why did he think it was so funny?* I used to run away from him each time, but he'd make a game of it by chasing me down. Eventually I resigned myself to just sitting and taking it. I learned that if I didn't react, he gave up fairly quickly. Yet every second of it made me hate him. It made me hate myself. *What was wrong with me?*

I looked at my wet face in the mirror. I gritted my teeth and studied my expression. I tried to look angry like him. I tried to look mean and scary. But it was just *me*, pretending. I didn't look angry or mean or scary. I just looked sad and weak.

Forming a fist with my right hand, I brought it up hard against my cheek. It hurt terribly, but something about the pain felt good. I did it again. And again. After a few punches I noticed my cheek getting pink and puffy, so I stopped.

My father once told me that if you ever wanted to punch someone where a bruise wouldn't show, do it in the stomach. So I clenched my stomach muscles and punched at myself with both hands, over and over again until I was exhausted from swinging. I had been holding my breath to be careful not to make any noise, so I grabbed a hand towel to muffle my exhale. After drying my face and hands, I folded the towel back up in thirds, the way he liked it, and placed it neatly over the towel bar.

Gathering my composure, I walked into the kitchen, where my mother stood pointing to the small wooden dinette set against the wall.

"Have a sandwich. There's some potato chips on the counter."

"Can I eat outside?" I asked softly.

"Well," she hesitated, studying my expression, "okay. But stay on the front porch."

I grabbed a sandwich and quickly walked to the door. Trying not to make even the slightest sound, I opened the door and slipped outside. The sun beat down on my face as I lowered myself onto the wooden steps of the porch. I could hear birds chirping merrily and the rustle of leaves, with branches swaying gently in the hot, July breeze. *Shhhh*, the trees seemed to say. *Shhhh*.

I took my sandwich and flung it as far as I could into the nearby shrubs. Then I lay down, drew my knees into my chest, and cried until the wind and the sun and the trees consoled me to sleep.

When twilight neared, I went upstairs to my bedroom. I kneeled by the window just in time to watch the sun sink into the lake. Upon the blanket of night appeared tiny specks of sparkling beauty, so slowly, glistening one by one. I watched until the night sky was filled with its perfect diamonds. I finally fell asleep waiting to make a wish on a falling star. I never saw one.

The next morning I awoke with a terrible pain in my neck. It took a second or two to figure out why I was slumped under the window and still wearing clothes from the day before.

Remembering that this was the morning of our row across the lake, I sat up and studied the shimmering water. How far was it to the other side? I strained to see anything, any landform across the great expanse of water. Nothing. Suddenly, it didn't seem like such a good idea to go to the other side in a rowboat.

I heard the toilet flush in the common bathroom between my room and the master bedroom. My father was awake. My mother would never have dared flush the toilet while he was sleeping. I quickly changed into some fresh clothes and made my way downstairs. The living room was still and quiet. I savored the few brief moments of silence before the day began. Rubbing my hands over the smooth fabric of an overstuffed burgundy chair, I scanned the room for something to occupy my time. On the mantel were a few books placed between a matching pair of carved bookends. The bookends were in the fashion of a captain's wheel positioned on a large wooden block. A few ragged, sun-bleached books lay between them, seemingly more for decoration than anything else. One book in particular caught my attention. It was a small, thin, blue book of poetry.

We occasionally studied poetry in school, and I enjoyed it immensely. The first time my teacher had recited verses to our class, I was instantly entranced. I felt an almost tangible connection with the poet and his feelings. While some words were difficult to understand, I just sort of knew what they meant. I could tell by the *feeling* of the poem—the rhymes and comparisons—so many beautiful ways to describe such simple things.

I had written a few poems myself. My teachers said they were fine, but none of them compared to those I heard. When I shared them with my father, he would laugh.

*You better stick to baseball, Shakespeare.*

I took down the book and examined its cover. *One Hundred and One Famous Poems.*

Settling down into the chair, I flipped through the pages and read a couple of lines from each poem. A few were beyond my comprehension, while others I just plain disliked.

I abruptly paused at one that intrigued me, written by William Ernest Henley back in the nineteenth century. It was titled "Invictus." I read the poem again and again, silently absorbing it. Then I read it aloud:

*Out of the night that covers me,*
*Black as the Pit from pole to pole,*
*I thank whatever gods may be*
*For my unconquerable soul.*

*In the fell clutch of circumstance*
*I have not winced nor cried aloud.*
*Under the bludgeonings of chance*
*My head is bloody, but unbowed.*

*Beyond this place of wrath and tears*
*Looms but the horror of the shade,*
*And yet the menace of the years*
*Finds, and shall find me, unafraid.*

*It matters not how strait the gate,*
*How charged with punishments the scroll,*
*I am the master of my fate;*
*I am the captain of my soul.*

Stumbling over a few words and becoming entangled in the unfamiliar cadence of others, I let the meaning settle deep within my being. I figured that William Ernest Henley must have been hurt a lot in his life, maybe by a father like mine.

"Who are you talking to?" my mother asked, peering around the room.

"No one," I said, tucking the book under the cushion.

"I'm gonna start breakfast. Make sure you fluff your seat before he gets down here and sees it all messed up," she warned, disappearing into the kitchen.

I jumped up and patted the cushion, removing any sign that it had been used. When I was certain no one was looking, I retrieved the book from the confines of the chair and returned it to the mantel. Entering the kitchen, I found a seat at the small table and waited for breakfast to be served.

A few moments later my father bounded into the room. When he was settled at the table, my mother placed a cup of steaming coffee in front of him, along with his pack of cigarettes topped off with a lighter. He pulled out a cigarette, tapped it on the table, and then looked at me.

"You hungry?" he asked, lighting the cigarette.

After a long inhale, he sat back and slowly released the smoke.

"Yeah," I said.

I hadn't eaten since we left our house the morning before, and I almost wished that I hadn't tossed the sandwich into the woods.

"Got some eggs and bacon," my mother chimed in.

"And toast?" he asked between sips.

"No," she said softly. "I forgot the bread on the table at home."

She placed a cup of coffee in front of me and quickly returned to the stove. Eggs were sizzling noisily in one frying pan, while the bacon popped and spattered in another.

"A lot of good that does me here. You knew I wanted toast," he scolded.

"I must have left my head on the counter, too," she kidded.

"Don't get cute," he said, raising his voice. "While we're out on the boat, you go pick some up at a convenience store or something."

"Okay," she agreed as she loaded his plate and handed it to him. "Here, hon. Sorry about the toast."

"I'm the one who's sorry," he snapped, mashing his cigarette butt into the ashtray.

After we finished eating, my father rose from the table.

"I'm gonna change my sweatshirt," he said. "Then we'll walk down to the dock."

He returned wearing a cream-colored sweatshirt, a pair of white shorts with white knee-high socks, and a pair of white tennis shoes. He changed his shirts often—two, three, sometimes even four times a day. He said he felt dirty or the sweatshirt didn't smell right.

Once outside, the three of us followed a path that cut around the side of the cabin and led to the lake. A choir of birds seemed to be singing their hellos as we passed, and from all around, melodic calls could be heard from the trees above.

"Do you know what kind of bird that is?" I asked after hearing a high-pitched trill.

"It's a red-footed shit sucker," my father laughed.

"No, really," I persisted.

"It's a red-footed shit sucker, I said. Isn't it, Les?" He turned to my mother for confirmation.

"Yep. That's what it sounds like to me," she said thoughtfully.

"There's no such thing," I argued.

"Well, maybe it's a three-headed wobble weaver. A distant relative of the pin-headed Leslie Weaver," he said, breaking into laughter.

"Oh, you dickhead," she said with a half-hearted attempt to slap his arm.

"Are you going on the rowboat, too?" I turned to ask her.

"No, you guys go ahead. I just wanted to see the lake. Then I'll go do a little shopping."

"Let's hope we beat the rush and can still get a rowboat," my father remarked as his pace quickened. The steep downward slope finally revealed a weathered boathouse bordering a long wooden dock. Parked alongside the dock were several rowboats, bobbing up and down with the gentle motion of the water.

When we approached, a gray-haired man popped out of the boathouse to greet us.

"How ya doin'?" he asked cheerfully. "Got plenty of boats this morning. You guys lookin' to do a little fishin'?"

"No," my father answered, shaking the man's hand. "I'm Dave St. Clair. This is my wife, Leslie, and my son, Chip. We—Chip and I, that is—just wanted to row around the lake a bit."

"Sure, sure," the man said, nodding. "I'll get you both life vests." He went inside, and then emerged from the boathouse with two bright-orange, puffy vests.

"Do you know how to put this on?" the man asked me. "Here, let me help you," he said as he slipped the vest over my head.

After fastening a few buttons and snaps, he stepped back to admire his work.

"There. That looks about right. How about you?" he asked, holding out the other vest.

"I'm fine," my father said, grabbing it from him. "I'll put it on in the boat."

"You really should put it on now. Why, I saw a guy get . . ."

"I said I'm fine," he interrupted. "I'll do it later."

My father turned abruptly and walked down the dock. I ran after him to catch up when he suddenly stopped dead in his tracks, causing me to plow face first into his back.

"Gotta watch that, ya know?" he chuckled.

"You did that on purpose," I said, rubbing my nose.

He ignored me and proceeded a bit farther down the row of boats. The wooden planks swayed slightly under our weight as we crossed them. Seeing a boat he liked, he climbed in and tossed the life vest down.

"Here," he gestured, holding out his hand.

I stepped in uneasily and almost lost my balance as he began rocking the boat.

"Don't fall in," he warned playfully.

"Now you guys be careful," my mother said as she looked down at us from the dock. "And you keep that vest on."

"Okay," I said, sitting down.

My father untied the loose knot that held the boat to the post. Grabbing the oars, he positioned them in the oarlocks, and used one to push us away from the dock toward the lake. When we had drifted free of the dock area, he began rowing at a steady pace. I watched the motion of the oars cutting through the water and felt a small splash each time he plunged them deep into the dark lake. We rowed along the shore for a while, passing an empty floating raft that had been anchored for swimmers to dive from. Looking over my shoulder, I saw the dock getting smaller and smaller. My mother's figure was barely visible, but I thought I could see her waving. I waved back.

Using only one oar, my father turned the boat perpendicular to the shore and then resumed rowing.

"Is it hard to row?"

"No, it's really good exercise. I'd like to have one of those rowing machines at home," he said between strokes.

We sat in silence for quite some time until we entered a larger body of water. The shoreline had broken away from the small inlet, and the full glory of the lake lay before us.

"You can take that off," he scoffed with a nod at my life vest. "You're a good swimmer. That's just for dumb-asses who can't swim."

Feeling proud that he had acknowledged my swimming abilities, I unfastened my vest. I knew I was a good swimmer. "Like a fish," people commented.

I thought back to an incident that had happened when I was about five years old and my parents were managing an apartment complex in Bloomfield Hills, Michigan. The summer sun was sinking into the western sky; I had been at the complex's pool practically all day. My father came to close up, and when the last of the swimmers had left, he told me to remove my floaties so he could teach me how to swim.

*Would I let you drown?* he asked.

I let the plastic floaties fall to the ground as he picked me up and carried me to the deep end of the pool.

*Ready?* he asked, suspending me over the water.

Before I could protest, he tossed me in. I sank down until my feet touched the bottom of the pool. I remember looking up and feeling my eyes burn from the chlorine as I took in the span of water between me and the surface. Panicking, I flapped my arms and legs in vain. Suddenly, I remembered the only thing I knew how to do—doggy-paddle. Slowly and methodically I cupped my hands and paddled while kicking my feet, and eventually I gained enough momentum to break through the surface with a triumphant gasp. Beaming, I paddled all the way around the deep end, deeming myself one of the greatest swimmers of all time.

*Hey, look at that. You're swimming,* he chuckled. *I told you that you wouldn't drown.*

He was right. I didn't drown. In fact, I quickly became a very good swimmer—better than most kids my age. I especially loved being underwater. Something about the silence and the seclusion below the surface comforted me. But that was only in a swimming pool, not in this dark, undulating body of water, which seemed to stretch out forever. Not knowing how deep it was made me even more uneasy.

"How deep is the lake?" I asked, peering down at my reflection.

"Not sure," my father said, bringing the boat to a halt. "Some say that parts of Lake Michigan are so deep they're immeasurable."

The sun was making its long journey through the sky as it peeked over the tightly packed forest along the shore. I couldn't see the dock anymore.

"You scared?" he asked.

"It's just that we're really far out," I said, swallowing the fear rising into my throat.

"You wanna swim?" he asked, putting down the oars.

"No, that's okay," I answered quickly.

"Chickenshit," he snorted. "It's only water. What, are you afraid of a little water?"

"No, I'm just not used to a lake yet. Maybe I'll swim closer to shore," I offered, attempting to mask the pleading tone in my voice.

As I was talking, he scooted over to me and put a large hand on my shoulder.

"I think you need to face your fears," he said gravely as he lowered his eyes to mine.

"No! I don't want to. Not now. I promise I'll swim later! Please, Dad! Plea—"

Jerking me out of my seat, he grunted as he threw me from the boat. I plunged headfirst into ice-cold water as chills shocked me to the very core. I began treading water immediately, panicked as I strained to see the rest of my body in the dark, murky water. My denim shorts instantly absorbed the water and began weighing me down, and my flip-flops were bobbing beside me. My T-shirt had gathered a pocket of air, causing it to float around my head.

I spun frantically in all directions, searching for the boat. I finally spotted it about twenty feet away, with my father rowing steadily toward the shore.

"Dad," I cried, "Dad, wait!"

In an effort to make swimming easier, I patted down the large pockets of air in my T-shirt. The boat came to a halt when I was about five feet away. My father had a familiar, taunting smile on his face.

"Come on, you'll have to do better than that," he goaded.

Biting his lip, he bent down to grab the oars.

As he rowed away, I hollered to him, "Dad, please wait! I'm trying!"

Once again, he rowed about twenty or thirty feet from me and watched me struggle to reach him. Salty tears were mixing with lake water as I lifted one arm over the other again and again.

When I was just within reach of the boat, he called to me.

"That's all you got? You got a long way to go, bud!"

"Please," I begged. "I'm getting tired! I'm going to drown. Let . . . me . . . on!"

I battled the water as I fought for breath, the frigid temperature stabbing at my lungs and sapping my strength. I heard the plunge of the oars into the water and looked up to see him putting more distance between us. I kept telling myself that if I could go on just a little farther, I could make it. *Focus on the boat. A few more feet, a few more feet, a few more. . . .*

Catching up to the rowboat once again, I heard him say, "See ya later, alligator."

I didn't waste my breath trying to call to him. I realized he was playing a very scary game. Instead I kept my pace, hoping he would show mercy. But he didn't. The rowboat became smaller and smaller until it blended in with the shoreline. I stopped swimming and began treading water. Shivering, I tried to get my bearings while I removed my T-shirt to lighten the load. The sun warmed the droplets on my face as I resumed swimming.

*The sun. That would be my destination.* I decided to swim for the sun, beyond the wall of trees. It almost seemed to be caressing me, comforting me. After a while, my arms grew tired, leaving me no alternative but to roll onto my back and kick. I turned around to study the shoreline, with the sun now just above the treetops. Disheartened by the distance I still had to travel, I wondered if this was how I was to die. My body was freezing and ached terribly. My arms and legs were growing ever more numb and harder to move.

*I'm going to drown,* I conceded.

As I struggled alone in Lake Michigan, contemplating death and the end of all I knew, my mind was graced by a thought. I remembered "Invictus":

> *I thank whatever gods may be*
> *For my unconquerable soul.*

*No, I will not die here,* I decided resolutely. *My soul will not die now.*

I felt a burst of energy, and I began kicking and paddling harder than before. Removing my shorts to reduce the drag, I tried to recall more of the poem.

*My head is bloody, but unbowed.*

Taking long, deep breaths, I developed a rhythm that matched the motion of my limbs. I continued to swim on and on, focusing on the poem and the sun.

*And yet the menace of the years*
*Finds, and shall find me, unafraid.*

I dove underwater and straightened my arms out at my sides. When I reached the surface, a faint glint in the distance caught my eye. The object was quite far from the shore, but I instinctively headed for it. Only a few yards away, I looked up to see an aluminum ladder fastened to the side of the floating raft we had passed on the way out. As I drew nearer, my heart leapt with happiness and renewed vigor. I resumed my rhythm and struggled toward my destination. The small wooden island floated steadily, awaiting my arrival. The sun had reflected off the silvery metal rail and guided me to safety. When I finally reached the ladder, I mumbled the final lines of the poem:

*I am the master of my fate,*
*I am the captain of my soul.*

I slumped down on the raft, exhausted yet exhilarated, and raised my head to see how far I had come. It was difficult to tell, but my muscles would attest that it had been a very long way. I lay in my underwear, shivering, and let the sun dry my body beneath the clear blue, cloudless sky.

"Hey," a voice echoed. "Hey, Chip, over here."

I wearily lifted myself onto my elbows and scanned the shoreline. Directly across from me, on a small sandy beach I hadn't noticed before, stood my father with his hands cupped around his mouth. Having caught my attention, he began waving me over. My muscles trembled in protest, but I stood up and climbed back down the aluminum ladder. The water grew clearer and shallower as I neared the shore, and eventually my legs met the sand below. Emerging from the water, I held my arms across my chest, shaking uncontrollably.

"Hey, good job!" my father said, slipping his arm around my neck as he steered me toward a wooded path. "The old bastard at the dock wondered what happened to you, and I told him you were a hell of a swimmer. I said, 'You just watch. Chip loves to swim.'"

I looked over in the direction of the dock to see the gray-haired man. He waved a wide arc back and forth with his entire arm.

"He's waving to us," my father said, smiling and waving.

He glanced down at me as we continued walking and then gave my shoulder a squeeze.

"I *said* he's waving to us. Wave," he demanded.

I raised my arm for the man to see. Apparently satisfied, he lowered his arm and walked back into the boathouse.

"There," my father said, watching the man close the door behind him. "There. Now let's go back and tell your mom what a great swimmer you are. Think she'll be pissed you lost all your goddamn clothes?" He laughed, poking me in the ribs.

"I don't know," I answered, staring at my bare feet as I gingerly stepped over the rocks and leaves littering the trail.

"Did your willy shrivel up in that cold water?" he asked as he reached out and grabbed my genitals through my wet underwear. I didn't flinch but instead kept trudging along.

During the remainder of the walk to the cabin, my father kept complimenting my swimming abilities, insisting that he was going to tell my mother how much fun we had had. He went on to relay stories about how he, too, had been a good swimmer when he was younger. After a while I blocked out his drivel, as my mind wandered to thoughts of a warm bath and a soft bed. I don't know how I was still able to walk. My legs felt like the heavy fallen logs that I saw all around me.

My mother was just pulling up to the cabin as we came up the path from around the side. She brought the car to a stop and quickly got out.

"What happened?" she asked, noticing my almost nude body, shaking and wet.

"Oh, nothing," he began. "He decided to go for a swim. Swam so fast he flew out of his clothes. Right, partner?"

"R-r-right," I stammered through chattering teeth. "C-can I take a b-bath?"

"Sure, honey. I'll go draw the water right away," she said, rubbing my back.

"You should have seen him, Les. Swam like a fucking dolphin," he boasted.

I stayed in my room for the rest of the day. The next morning, as my parents loaded up the car, I slipped back inside the cabin. When no one was watching, I snuck over to the mantel and grabbed the book of poetry. Pushing the bookends back together to conceal the empty space, I tucked the book inside my jeans. I was sure no one would miss it. To the owners of the cabin it was merely a decoration.

To me it was a secret treasure.

"Mr. St. Clair?" a voice echoed.

I caressed the thin, blue poetry book, remembering the grainy texture of its cover as it had felt in my hands so many years before.

"Mr. St. Clair? Do you need a break? Some water maybe?"

I raised my eyes to find the head of the parole board motioning to a clerk.

"I'm fine," I said, breathing out a deep sigh.

Leaning down, I slipped the book back into the leather attaché case, not realizing that I had removed it while I was talking.

I noticed that the once-intense gazes seemed a little less intense, less scrutinizing. One of the board members laced her fingers, placing her hands on the table.

"I understand how difficult this must be for you. If you need to stop . . ." she said, offering a slight smile.

"The difficulty was in living it, not in telling it."

A nod told me she understood. I watched her reach for a pen to resume taking notes as the head of the parole board addressed me.

"Before you begin again, I have a question. Weren't there any good times in your childhood? I mean your memories—don't you have any positive recollections?"

"It's hard to remember any time, any day that wasn't somehow . . ." I paused, searching for the correct word, "tainted."

"Explain," he said coldly.

I looked at the other board members as I spoke. The gray-haired man, Mr. Penfold, seemed too closed to hear what I was saying.

"If I offered you a glass of milk—ice cold, fresh milk—and watched you drink it down until the glass was empty, what would your response be when I asked you how you liked it? You would probably smile and tell me what a great glass of milk it was. But if I told you, while the milk mustache was still drying on your lip, that I actually had some contagious, life-threatening disease and had spit into the glass before you drank it, what would be your response then?"

I returned my eyes to Mr. Penfold and said, "Would you still claim that the milk was great, now that you knew its secret? You may not have been able to taste a difference, but that betrayal undermined whatever enjoyment you would have gotten out of the milk. Because of your newfound knowledge, the taste of the milk had been tainted."

The board member to the far right, who looked younger than the others, shuffled uncomfortably in his chair.

"I think we understand . . ." he began, but Mr. Penfold interrupted.

"Yes, but what about holidays, birthdays? Surely it wasn't all tainted."

I turned my head and looked over my right shoulder at my fiancée Lisa. She gave me a loving glance, then lowered her head.

Reaching back into the black leather case at my feet, I retrieved the small, pale-green sheet of paper and placed it in front of me.

"Do any of you know the significance of the date August first?" I asked, scanning the panel.

"That was the day your fath—Michael Grant committed the murder," answered the young board member.

"That's right," I said, lifting up the green birth certificate and turning it around so all could see. "But coincidentally, it is also the day I was born."

# CHAPTER
# 4

# Sanctuary

As a child, I believed birthdays were magical, even mystical, for your birthday was the one day each year you could feel special. Although I had never known such a day, I woke up every single birthday with the hope that this one would be different.

Jumping out of bed, I pulled on a new pair of shorts and a T-shirt and tiptoed to the door. I wasn't sure if anyone was awake yet so I had to be quiet. As I crossed the hall and headed toward the stairway, I heard water running in the bathroom adjacent to my parents' bedroom. The salty smell of bacon, the sounds of sizzling and popping, told me that my mother was already downstairs preparing breakfast, so I gathered it must have been my father in the bathroom. I rarely entered my parents' bedroom: It was a family rule not to go rummaging through the house. Even a search for something as innocuous as a bath towel would spark a hissing warning from my mother: "Ask me if you need something. Don't just go rummaging around!"

But on this day, a rare surge of curiosity compelled me to steal a peek into my parents' bedroom.

Tracing my way toward the bathroom at the far left corner, I carefully stepped over the lines in the carpet left by the vacuum. Peering into the small room, I saw my father's reflection in the mirror above the sink. He scrubbed vigorously at his mouth with a toothbrush, his hand a blur as he stared down at the running water. Without so much as a change in the rhythm of his hand, his eyes lifted and caught mine in the mirror, holding them fast. My body felt a violent rush of electricity, but I managed a smile.

"Hey, birthday boy," he mumbled through foamy lips. "Do you feel older?"

"Not really," I said, moving into the doorway.

He removed the toothbrush and, with his other hand, cupped the running water and ran it over his mouth. I noticed that his pale skin was stretched with extra weight and folded at the waist over the tight elastic band of his black briefs. His normally neat and combed dark hair was in disarray and ruffled from sleep.

As he turned to face me, I saw the long scar that went from the top of his stomach all the way down to the elastic on his underwear. He followed my eyes and looked down.

"Got this one in Vietnam," he said proudly.

"I know. Did it hurt?"

"Hell, yeah, it hurt! Did ya think it felt good?"

"No," I answered, putting my head down.

"It was my first tour. I was a Green Beret, ya know. We got ambushed and they zippered me. Seven shots. Everyone got hit. I laid there for days. I was the only one who survived. A Marine Recon group found me. Next thing I knew, I woke up in Tripler Hospital in Honolulu." He kneeled down and looked me straight in the eyes. "Then I went back for revenge," he growled.

He tipped his head and fingered a dent on his scalp.

"See that?" he asked, his voice distressed.

"Yeah."

"Touch it," he insisted. "Those fuckers got me again. That time I wasn't so lucky, ya know?"

"Yeah," I said again as I lightly placed my finger against the shallow dent in his skull.

You couldn't see it until you really got down and looked for it. But there it was, a dent about the size of a marble. Sometimes I wondered if getting shot in the head made him get mean.

He stood back up and looked at me, his eyes brimming with tears.

"They got to me before the Recon group that time," he began slowly, his eyes seeing through me to another place, another time, very far away. "They held me prisoner for six months, putting me through the worst torture you could imagine. Someday, I'll tell you more. You're too young now." He wiped his eyes and let out a deep breath.

"Why do you get me talking about all this shit?" he asked with a half-cocked smile.

He dropped his hand on my head and tousled my hair as I shrugged.

"I'm gonna hop in the shower now. Is Mom making breakfast?" he asked, sliding the shower door on its track with a soft rumble.

"Yeah," I answered, turning around. "I'm going down now."

Upon entering the kitchen, I found my mother seated at the small oak dinette with the phone pressed to her ear. She looked up and pursed her lips tightly together in an effort to smile. She laughed and nodded in response to whoever was on the other end of the line, then reached for a can of beer. She closed her eyes and took a long, deep gulp. Her neck was covered in bruises, which she tried to conceal with makeup. The shade she used had transformed the bright purple marks into soft, dark-brown spots. As I studied them, she placed the beer can back on the table and brought her hand up to her throat in an effort to block my view. My gaze shifted to the puffy blue and yellow bruises around her left eye, then to the two empty beer cans under the windowsill.

"Chip's right here, Chris. Wanna talk to him?" I heard her say into the phone.

It was my Aunt Christine, my father's sister who lived in Indiana.

"I have to get back to breakfast," my mother said, rising from her seat and handing me the phone.

"Hi, Aunt Chris." I pushed back the chair with my foot and sat down.

"Hi, honey," she said merrily. "Do you know what day it is today?"

"Yeah, it's August first," I answered, intentionally avoiding the response she wanted.

"Well, I know that," she chuckled. "It's also your birthday. Happy birthday!"

"Yeah, thanks," I said, trying to bring some sort of emotion into my voice to match her mood.

"We sent something along for you. You probably won't get it for a couple of days; maybe Thursday," she added.

"Great, I'll watch for it."

"Is everything okay, honey?"

"Yeah."

My mother was studying my expression, trying to figure out the other side of the conversation. Seeing my opportunity, I quickly ended the phone call.

"Mom's here, Aunt Chris. I think she wants to talk to you now. See ya."

Passing the phone back to my mother, I left the kitchen and headed toward the basement. Like the rest of the apartment, the basement was fully furnished. It was carpeted with soft gray Berber with imitation wood paneling on the walls that gave the large space a warm, comfortable feel. Homey as the walls were, though, they were missing something—something that adorned the walls of the friends' and neighbors' homes I visited.

Returning to the kitchen, I approached my mother as she hung up the phone.

"Hey, Mom, where are my baby pictures?"

"What do you mean?" she asked, turning her attention to the food on the stove.

"Baby pictures, birthday pictures of me. Wedding pictures of you. Where are they?"

"Huh? Well, we move so much that everything is still packed away in boxes."

That was possible. We did move an awful lot. We had already moved five or six times that I could remember.

"By the time I'd have everything unpacked, we'd probably move again. Ya know?" Gliding back toward me, she punched me in the arm.

"Ow!" I moaned, recoiling from her.

"Oh, you pussy," she mocked, sticking out her tongue.

Massaging the pain in my arm, I turned toward the basement door once again, when suddenly I smelled a foul odor.

After a few deep breaths, I realized that it was coming from the hall bathroom. I turned the knob and leaned my head into the sink, sniffing to no avail. The toilet behind me was the only other possible source, so I grimaced and reluctantly opened the lid.

"Ugh." Someone had obviously used it but failed to flush, so I reached my hand out and pressed the handle.

"Nooo!" my mother yelled from the kitchen.

Before the toilet even finished its entire flush cycle, she was at the door.

"Chip! Damn it, why did you do that? You knew he was taking a shower," she cried.

I spun around and looked at her face. Her half-angry, half-panicked expression changed to one of total panic as a blood-curdling scream filled the air.

"Aaahhhh! Motherfucker! Ahhh!" we heard as we stared at each other, too scared to move.

"You *know* that flushing the toilet causes all the cold water to leave the shower! He's probably burnt like a lobster," she moaned, now pacing back and forth.

"I-I forgot," I stuttered.

"Who's the motherfucker that burnt me?!" he roared as the shower shut off.

I heard him mumbling and stomping around upstairs.

"Whoever it was, is dead! Dead!"

"Oh, God, Chip. Oh, God," she murmured.

My eyes darted to the front door. I thought of running. I had no idea where I'd go, but anywhere would have been better than where I was. She must have read my mind because she placed her hand on my shoulder.

"No," she sighed. "It'll only make things worse. Here he comes."

My entire body trembled so violently that I thought I might faint. His wet bulk rushed down the stairs like a crazed animal ready to lash out at anything in its path. His eyes were wide and angry, the corners of his mouth turned down in a fierce scowl. Aside from the terrifying expression, all he wore was a bath towel wrapped around his large waist.

"Dave," she pleaded, "he didn't mean to. I went to the bath-room earlier and . . ."

Without looking at her, he placed his hand on her face and pushed her into the kitchen. She fell back and crouched silently, watching.

His eyes were focused on me, and I could do little else but shake. I couldn't breathe; I couldn't speak. When he finally reached me, looming and dark, I only managed a squeak.

"Please."

"You stupid little cocksucker!" he yelled. "You little fuck. You were trying to kill me, weren't you?"

He grabbed me by the upper arms and jerked me into the air. Petrified, I stared at him with my mouth open. I was too afraid to cry.

"I have third-degree burns, you piece of shit," he raged as he shook me.

My head flopped back and forth, causing me to bite my tongue. His eyes revealed a tremendous loathing as he contin-ued to shake me. Letting out an unintelligible scream, he spun me around, slamming me into the front door. My body hit with such force that I lost my breath, while my head snapped back and rammed against the hardwood. It felt as if all my back teeth had broken into pieces. Then, just when I thought I couldn't endure another moment, he dropped me. I crumpled to the floor and scooted into the corner, bringing my knees up to my chest. He turned around and went back upstairs. As usual, as suddenly as the violence had erupted, it subsided.

"You okay?" my mother whispered as she peered in from the doorway.

I pressed both hands against the top of my head, which felt like it might split wide open. Tasting fresh blood in my mouth, I began to sob.

"Oh, don't cry," she warned. "That will really piss him off. Get up and eat something. Shit, you got off pretty easy," she said, raising her finger to the yellowish bruise on her cheekbone.

I stared at her, clenching my jaw and choking back tears.

*Don't cry,* I thought. *Don't let her see you cry.*

Willing myself not to let one teardrop fall, I bent down, grabbed my sneakers from the doormat, threw open the front door, and ran outside.

My heart was pounding in time with the rhythm of my shoeless feet as I got farther and farther away. Losing the battle as I ran on, tears began to stream down my face. When I made a sharp turn around the back of a building, I stumbled upon a group of kids playing baseball in a parking lot. I backed up behind the building and melted into the shadows. I didn't feel like seeing anyone.

Slipping my sneakers on, I crossed the street and ran alongside the shrubbery, ducking down to remain unseen. I felt the wind and the sun around me as I neared my destination. I could see it just ahead: the old, wooden gazebo that sat atop a small, grassy hill in a vast field—my hiding place ever since we moved to this town. Spotting my sanctuary, I ran faster to reach it. The gray paint was flaking from years of exposure to harsh weather.

The rotten wood splintered in several places. But to me it was a castle. My fortress. I often went there when life at home became too much to bear. I'd crawl under the gazebo, smelling the earth and the grass amidst the scattered wood chips, tucking myself deep within. The world passed me by, oblivious to my existence. I lay there for hours, the solitude and peace comforting my soul. Sometimes I would bring a book and lose myself within its pages. My sanctuary provided a cool shade and my books a soft breeze in the scorching heat of reality.

I looked up to see the sun glowing through the treetops on the blazing hot summer's day. My birthday. If I could have made a wish, the magical kind that only comes true on birthdays, I would have wished for a gentle rain.

# CHAPTER
## 5

# A Winter
# Foreshadowing

PRESSING MY HEAD AGAINST the cold bus window, I looked out at the blanket of pure white that had covered Bloomfield Hills over the past few hours. It was just before noon on Friday, and school had let out for Christmas break after only a half-day.

*No more school 'til after the New Year,* I thought, as I watched the large white snowflakes flutter slowly to the ground.

Of all the seasons, I liked winter best. The silence in the snow all around, the absence of almost any sign of life somehow made everything seem so completely peaceful. No noise except the crunching of snow beneath my feet.

As we left the bus, groups of kids were grabbing handfuls of the sloppy slush and pelting one another in an effort to start a snowball fight. Although it seemed like fun to join them, I kept to myself; I had to get home and call my mother to let her know where I was.

Leaning down toward the door lock, I removed the house key from under my sweater and plugged it into the keyhole. Kicking off my boots, I stepped into the kitchen and proceeded toward the phone.

"Hunters Ridge Apartments. Can I help you?" my mother said pleasantly.

"Hi, Mom."

"Oh, hi, hon. That's right," she said, apparently remembering why I was calling so early. "You had a half-day."

"Yeah," I said, "the teacher sent us home with a paper for you guys to read. I'll put it on the kitchen table."

"Okay," she said, her voice fading as she turned from the phone to talk to someone in the background. "Hey, Chip, Dad's on his way home. He wants to talk to you."

"Okay," I said, concerned. "I'll show him what the teacher sent."

I figured it might distract him from whatever it was he was going to tell me.

As soon as I hung up the phone, I rushed to the front door to straighten my boots and find the paper the teacher had sent home. I positioned it neatly on the kitchen table, then bolted into the living room to check for anything that might look out of order. Everything seemed to be all right. Pillows fluffed, carpet vacuumed, books and magazines stacked neatly. Expecting him at any time, I sat down at the kitchen table and reviewed the notice my fifth-grade teacher passed around:

Dear Parents,

Your child's safety is one of our highest priorities. In an effort to protect your child, we are suggesting that you create a password that only you and your child know. This password can be given to anyone you trust to pick up your child in your absence. Anyone who is unable to provide the correct password will be unable to pick up your child. Be sure to practice so that he/she remembers the correct password. If we all work together, we can ensure our children's safety and well-being.

Sincerely,
Eagle Elementary School

Just as I finished reading, my father arrived. He stepped out of his shoes and leaned into the kitchen with a big smile.

"Hi. No more school, huh?"

"Not for a while," I responded, getting up from my chair.

I walked to him and handed over the paper. He read it as he entered the kitchen, turning to me when finished.

"What do you think the password should be?"

"Um," I pondered, "how about *Green Beret*?"

"Ha," he threw back his head and laughed. "Good one. *Green Beret* it is."

I smiled at him, glad that he liked my suggestion.

"Hey," he said, pulling out his usual chair at the table, "you know Christmas is just around the corner."

"I know," I said, as I watched him reach back to pull out his red leather wallet.

Thumbing through it, he continued, "I haven't gotten a chance to do much shopping, what with work and all."

Several green bills unfolded in his hand, and then he returned his wallet to his back pocket.

"I'm trusting you to do my Christmas shopping for me," he said, flopping down the money in front of me.

"How much is it?" I asked, my eyes widening.

"Three hundred bucks. Now be careful with it—I'm trusting you. Remember, fuck this up and that's *it* between you and me, capeesh?" he finished, holding a hand out for me to shake.

"What should I get her?" I asked, shaking his hand.

Lacing his fingers in front of him, he mulled over my question.

"I was thinking some new pajamas, maybe a dress or two. Get something for her from yourself. And bring me the change," he warned with a wagging finger.

"Okay, I will," I said. "But what size do I get?"

"Shit, I don't know," he said, rolling his eyes. "Just find someone who looks about her size and ask."

"Oh, okay," I agreed reluctantly.

"Well, get goin'. Make sure to buy a card and some wrapping paper, too. Don't be too long now. Call if something happens."

He got up and strolled out of the room. Upon hearing him close the bedroom door, I ran to the phone.

"Hey, Mom," I whispered as soon as I heard her pick up. "Listen, Dad just gave me money to go Christmas shopping. Do I get something for him with this money?"

"Uh, something small, I suppose," she began. "I already picked up most of his gifts."

"Okay, gotta go. Bye," I said quickly and hung up the phone.

Grabbing the money, I divided it into four stacks as my mother had taught me. I stuffed one in each of my front pants pockets and placed one in each boot. Out of the house and down the road I headed, my feet sinking slightly into the snow as I neared the local shopping complex. I had been there many times before, sometimes taking my allowance to the arcade inside the shopping mall. For Father's Day and Mother's Day, I would trek there for presents. I had never before, however, had the unwelcome responsibility that now loomed before me. At most I was given $50 by my mother to shop for birthdays and other occasions. This time I had to be certain to get everything he had asked for and return the correct amount of change.

Once inside, I planned the best course of action. I figured I had better make certain to get the items he had requested first. Walking slowly by each of the brightly decorated shop windows, I scrambled to find a women's clothing store. I stumbled upon a glass display with a very sophisticated mannequin poised delicately with arms outstretched; she was wearing a black dress down to the floor, with a thick, red leather belt. The colors caught my eye, and I excitedly entered the store. After spending a few minutes struggling to find the rack that held the dress in the window,

I finally gave up and scouted around for a salesperson. An older woman with short blonde hair was placing sweaters on a small table. She cocked her head as she folded each one, trying to make them look just right. When she noticed me, she smiled.

"Hi, dear. Are you lost?" she asked warmly.

"No, I'm shopping. I want to buy that dress," I said, pointing to the display window at the front of the store.

"Oh," she said, taken aback. "Well, okay. Come this way."

I followed her to the back of the store. Near the cash register was a shiny metal rack holding several dresses similar to the one on the mannequin.

"Here we go. Is your mother here?" she asked, glancing behind me.

"No, she's at work. How much is it?"

"It's $49.95," she said, looking uncomfortable. "But how about your father?"

"He's at home. He gave me some money to go Christmas shopping with," I added proudly.

"It's just," she hesitated, "maybe you should find something a little more in your price range."

"Oh, no," I shook my head, "that's fine. I have it right here in my boot."

Shaking off the footwear, I dug inside and produced three $20 bills.

The saleswoman literally took a step backward and laughed.

"Okay," she said, raising her hands in the air in a mock protest. "I give up. What size does she wear?"

"Uh, about your size, I guess," I estimated, as I studied the woman's stature.

"Okay, then. Will there be anything else, sir?" she asked, taking the dress down from the rack.

"How about some warm pajamas?"

"Sure," she said with a grin. "Right here. These are really warm. They're flannel."

Stepping away from the counter, she leaned down to a nearby shelf and grabbed a soft-looking pair of lavender pajamas.

I stepped back into my boot and reached into my right front pocket for some additional money.

"That will be $96.90."

I handed her five $20 bills and placed the remainder back into my pocket. With a rip of the receipt, she gathered the correct change and placed it into my open palm.

"There you go. Now, you be careful. Merry Christmas!" she added as I pulled the bag off the counter.

I resumed my place in the large artery of flowing people being pumped by the heart of the holiday season. My stomach was growling so I headed to the food court. Confident that my father would not mind if I stopped for a bite to eat, I followed the aroma and decided on an old favorite—a cheeseburger from the Honey Tree. As I sat down to eat, I realized that I was the only kid my age without parents around, and I felt very privileged. As I finished off my meal, I leaned back to look into the arcade. I checked my watch and decided that it was time to do a little more shopping; I could play some video games if time permitted.

Browsing through several different stores, I bought my mother a fragile glass rose, which was tinted pink and green, and a top-of-the-line coffeepot that would apparently keep coffee warm for hours. For my father, I purchased a gold-plated lighter with a small button on the outside. When you touched the button, a flame appeared like magic. He had always hated flipping the little wheel on the small, cheap lighters. Then I entered a gift shop and bought several rolls of wrapping paper and ribbon, along with three Christmas cards. The load I was dragging was now almost bigger than I was, and I began to feel strange because I was drawing odd looks from passersby. But I had gotten everything he asked for. I hoped.

"I'm back!" I managed to breathe out as I shut our front door, huffing and puffing from the exertion of carrying all my packages several blocks.

"I'm in here," my father answered from the living room.

The glow of the television cast an eerie light on my father as he sat in his recliner.

"Want to see what I got?" I asked proudly, still trying to regain my wind.

"Hold on. I'm watching something," he snapped with a quick glance at me.

I stood there breathing shallowly as I waited.

"Dad, look," I said impatiently.

"What?" he glared down at my packages. "Yeah, great. Oh, Jesus Christ!"

Kicking the footstool under the chair, he leapt up and turned off the television.

"There, what is it?"

"I thought you'd want to see what I got," I pouted.

"I do, I do," he said, reaching into a bag. "Let's see. Not bad," he remarked, pulling the dress from the bag. "Nice pajamas. Now she can throw out those old raggedy fuckers."

I removed the remaining items from the bags, all except the lighter. I snuck that into my jacket pocket.

"Quite a haul, kid. Good job," he remarked, roughly patting my shoulder.

"I ate lunch, too," I added as soon as it crossed my mind.

"You did?" he asked, in mock disgust. "Well, where the hell is my change, big spender?"

I kicked off a boot and pulled out $60. In my pockets, I found another $13.70. I placed it in a pile on the end table next to him.

"Hey, Chip," he said, helping me gather the bags. "You know that letter from your school?"

"Yeah."

"Well, what would you do," he began slowly, "if you found out that you'd been kidnapped? That we'd kidnapped you."

*Kidnapped? Why would he ask me this?* "I don't know," I said, bewildered, as I walked ahead of him up the stairs. "That would be kind of weird."

"Yeah. What if you found out you were from some rich family or something? Would you forget about us?"

"Nah," I laughed. "Maybe I'd give *you* an allowance."

"Oh, you would, huh? Thanks a lot, Daddy Warbucks. Here,

help me wrap these," he said, dropping the gifts to the floor.

He was in a very strange mood. He didn't laugh at my joke, as I had expected, but he also didn't seem very serious. I dismissed the question as a shadow of a thought, meaningless and inconsequential. Yet I found in years to come that in the glaring light of truth, shadows always remain.

# CHAPTER 6

# Into the West

Dᴵᴰ ɪᴛ ᴇᴠᴇʀ ᴏᴄᴄᴜʀ to you to run away?"

The tone of his question and the stoic looks on the faces of the parole board members made it clear they still didn't understand.

How could I make them understand that I couldn't just *run away*? Why couldn't they see that I was trapped? The concrete and steel of the prison that surrounded me in that moment, with its scores of armed guards, held less sway over its inmates than my father held over me with a fierce eye. I was a child in the clutches of a vicious tyrant who ruled by terror.

"I couldn't," I answered, struggling to articulate everything surging through my mind.

Blank looks inspired me to try again.

"I had no frame of reference to realize that what I was going through wasn't normal," I explained. "And I was so afraid . . ."

I almost never spoke of the shades that still haunted me, even in daylight, when a smell or a sound would evoke a horrifying memory. Sometimes, catching the scent of the soap my father used, or hearing the metallic flip of a cheap lighter, brought me back to a place I desperately wanted to leave behind. Nighttime was even worse. I would wake up drenched in sweat, screaming like a madman. During the day, I never allowed myself to be alone with my own thoughts for long, for fear of remembering. I just kept busy. Reading, talking, working, anything.

I marveled at how Lisa could sit and watch the stars, a contented smile playing on her lips. I, on the other hand, had to fill every waking moment with some task or hobby—anything but writing. I had abandoned that as a teenager, fearing the deluge of pain that might burst onto the page. But now I needed to remember—to convey to these strangers the agony and fear that had been my life.

With a deep breath, I plunged into the darkness and opened yet another door.

I wanted to go to the gazebo one last time—something in my bones told me I'd never see it again—but my father never gave me the chance. We were packed and ready to go, moving for the seventh or perhaps the eighth time; I'd lost track.

The sky glowed a dusky pink in the early morning hours. We had gotten an early start as usual, waking up around 4:00 AM to drive through the Nevada desert before midday. My father explained that the sun could cause the car to overheat and break down. He had hoped to cross the California state line by noon and be in Orange County by 3:00 or 4:00 PM. My parents' friend in Orange County was storing the few boxes we had shipped beforehand. Once settled in, we'd retrieve our belongings.

I sat in my usual place behind the passenger seat, staring out the window at the palette of color streaking the sky. As the sun rose, a fiery pink mixed with a faint orange, creating a brilliant effect. I glanced out the back window and could still see glowing stars in the blue-black sky. Dawn seemed to be so mystical—the few moments before the world awakens yet still dreams. Dawn was a time when just about anything seemed possible, when something magnificent might happen. I watched as the sun ignited life all around, finding its way over the dusty, rust-colored plateaus. A few hours later, we passed through Las Vegas. To my young eyes, it didn't seem very glamorous. No lights, no bustling people, just a dusty town with a multitude of signs in the middle of nowhere.

I fell asleep watching the cacti sail by as we made our way down the highway, when suddenly a loud voice jolted me out of my slumber.

"Oh, Jesus Christ!" my father growled as his eyes caught hold of something in the rearview mirror.

I turned around to see the blue-and-red flashing lights atop a police car.

"Do you want me to switch with you?" my mother asked, sounding panicked.

"No, stay put," he snapped. "Let's just play it cool. Real cool. Chip, not a word," he warned.

We slowed and eventually came to a stop on the shoulder of the highway. The police car pulled in directly behind us, stopping a few feet away. An officer in a tan uniform got out and shut the door. He spat on the ground as he approached our car. My father rolled down the window and smiled as the officer leaned in to assess the car and its occupants.

"Hello, officer," my father said in a warm, friendly manner. "I might have been going a little fast back there. My son has to use a bathroom, and I was trying to make it to the next exit as quickly as possible."

"Driver's license," the officer stated simply.

"Uh," my father stumbled. "Well, you see . . . I'm a Vietnam vet. Green Beret Captain David Michael St. Clair. I did three tours over there. Left a lot of flesh and blood there, too. On my third tour, I took one to the knee."

I could see my father's eyes welling up with tears through the rearview, his voice shaking as he continued. "The doctor said I would never walk right again. I limped for a while and could never pass a driving test because the doctor had classified me as permanently disabled. I'm perfectly fine to drive—it's just military red tape, ya know?"

The police officer removed his dark sunglasses and nodded. "Yeah, well, I did a year over there myself, back in '61. Nothin' like what you went through, though. You're a lucky man to be in one piece after all that."

He leaned over to look at me, a big smile spreading across his face.

"Your dad's a hero," he said. "Like Rambo, huh?"

"Yeah, like Rambo."

"Okay, Captain St. Clair. I think you've earned the right to drive a car. Just slow down," he chuckled. "Y'all take care, now."

Returning his sunglasses to his face, he swaggered back to the squad car and got in. My father pulled back onto the road and breathed a sigh of relief.

"That was close," he said.

"You handled it great, honey," my mother assured him.

"Dad?"

"Yeah," he replied, checking his mirror.

"I thought you got shot in the knee on your first tour in Vietnam. You know, when you got shot in the stomach and the head."

"That's what I said. During the first tour."

"No, you didn't. You told the policeman that you got shot in the knee on the third tour."

"He said the first tour," my mother corrected.

"But—"

"Chip!" he shouted. "Enough! I was there; you weren't. Now shut the fuck up and read your stupid fucking books."

I slumped back into my seat as my father lit a cigarette, inhaling deeply with his head tipped back. Although I didn't feel much like reading, I picked up a book from the seat next to me and flipped it open. The rushing of air through the open window was the only sound for what seemed like hours as I stared blankly at the pages, until my father's voice broke through.

"California, here we are!" my father trumpeted. I looked up just in time to see the welcome sign as we sped by.

As my father had predicted, we entered Orange County around 3:00 PM. He pulled into a Hilton Hotel and proceeded to the unloading area.

"I'll go see if there are any vacancies," he said, putting the car into park. "You wanna come, Chip?"

"Sure," I said, eager to stretch my legs.

We entered the lobby through a revolving door. I felt overwhelmed by the large windows and palm trees scattered throughout.

A man behind a sprawling granite counter smiled as we approached. "May we help you?"

"Yeah, I'm Dr. St. Clair. We need a room for a few days."

I looked up, shocked at the word "doctor." My father stole a glance at me, and then shifted his eyes back to the man behind the counter.

"Certainly, just fill this out," he said, setting a pen next to a clipboard on the counter.

After a few moments, my father turned to me.

"Chip, go back to the car and tell your mom to come in. You stay out there."

"Okay," I said, heading for the revolving door.

"What's going on?" my mother asked as I crawled into the backseat.

"He wanted you to come inside," I said, retrieving the book I had been reading.

Shortly afterward, they came back to the car laughing.

"What's so funny?"

"Oh, nothing," my mother said, waving a hand. "We got a room."

We ended up staying at the hotel for about two weeks. My mother was busy lining up job interviews and scouring the newspaper for homes to rent. My father sat in front of the television from morning to night.

One day my mother bounded excitedly through the door and informed us that she had found a house in Anaheim. It was fully furnished and would suffice until we got on our feet. The next day, we moved into the small, brick, ranch-style house with a fireplace. The décor was neutral with a lot of creams and beiges.

California didn't seem very exciting to me, so I kept to my room, reading and rereading books and writing poems. I felt very out of place. But then again, I always felt out of place.

After a month or so, my parents landed a job in Long Beach as the managers of a high-rise apartment complex called International Towers. The first time I saw it, my jaw literally dropped. The building stretched thirty stories into the sky and was perfectly cylindrical. I had never seen anything like it.

We moved in on my eleventh birthday. When we got into the elevator, I looked at the numbers corresponding to all the floors.

"Which floor?" I asked my mother.

"Fourteen."

I found the number fourteen and pressed it. "Hey, there's no thirteenth floor!" I exclaimed.

"Whaddya know," my mother yawned.

"Well, technically we're on the *thirteenth* floor. I mean, they call it fourteen, but thirteen really comes after twelve."

My mother thought about it for a moment.

"You're right. I'm not unpacking everything then. We're moving to another floor. I'll talk to my boss tomorrow," she said, visibly shaken.

"Christ," my father said, "who gives a damn!"

"It's bad luck," she said simply. "We don't need any bad luck."

I turned to look at my father, expecting him to blow up at her stupid suggestion.

"Alright," he agreed.

My father, agreeing? While I always knew my mother was highly superstitious, I wasn't aware of my father being so. If it was one thing my father hated, it was a hassle, and moving to another apartment was a big one. As we rode the elevator in silence, I wondered just when had my father gotten so superstitious.

I started school in September. The kids in my class accepted me readily enough, and I made a couple of fairly good friends. But on one day in particular they were both sick, which left me alone. At lunchtime, instead of going to the cafeteria by myself, I headed for the library.

The room was practically empty except for the librarian, who sat behind a large wooden desk toward the back. I quietly placed my backpack on one of the desks and made my way through the walls of texts and treasures. Scanning the spines of the books, I came across a name I knew: William Shakespeare. I had read a few of his poems and had a deep appreciation for his work. Clasping the book, I strolled back to my place at the table, removed my lunch from my backpack, and opened the book. *Hamlet, Romeo and Juliet, Macbeth*. I chose *Hamlet*.

I became so enraptured with the words that I returned to the library each day during lunchtime to read more. My friends had long since returned to school, but I had found a new way to spend my lunch hour. I could feel the anguish and turmoil Hamlet held within his heart. When I stumbled upon his soliloquy, I studied it slowly and carefully:

> *To be, or not to be; that is the question;*
> *Whether 'tis nobler in the mind to suffer*
> *The slings and arrows of outrageous fortune,*
> *Or to take arms against a sea of troubles,*
> *And by opposing end them. To die: to sleep.*

Sandwich in hand, I read on, absorbing the printed words. Hamlet's father had been murdered in an underhanded effort to steal the crown. While Hamlet lay mourning, his father's spirit appeared before him, beckoning Hamlet to exact revenge upon his uncle, the murderer. In Hamlet's soliloquy, he wrestles with the unbearable task placed before him. Feeling like a coward for not being able to fulfill his father's final wishes, he contemplates suicide to relieve his agony.

At the end of his soliloquy, however, Hamlet realizes that the mystery surrounding the uncharted territory of death is even more troubling than his current dilemma.

"You know," a voice whispered from behind, "you can check that book out."

Startled, I spun around to see the librarian smiling at me.

"Oh, yes, ma'am. I know," I replied.

"I've watched you come in here every day for a while now, just reading away. I didn't know if you were aware that you could check the book out and take it home with you. For a period of time, of course," she added.

I had already made the mistake of bringing library books home. *What's this?* he'd say, snatching the book from my hand. *What a faggot! Why don't you play ball or something like normal kids, instead of burying your nose in this shit?*

"I'd prefer to read *here,* if you don't mind."

"No, not at all. What are you reading?" she asked.

"*Hamlet.*"

"Oh," she laughed, "at your age? Well, that's wonderful. What else do you like to read?"

I showed her the other book I was reading.

"Poetry, too, huh?"

"Yeah."

"Have you ever read Jules Verne or O. Henry?" she inquired, a light of fondness flickering in her eyes.

"No, do you like them?" I asked.

"Oh, yes, they were wonderful authors. Here," she beckoned me to follow her.

Examining the walls of books, she searched until she found the ones she was looking for. She handed them over and walked me back to my seat.

"You'll enjoy these very much," she beamed. "Just let me know if you need any more."

"I will. Thank you," I said, taking my seat again.

Looking around at all the books lining the walls, I wondered if it would take me an entire lifetime to read every one. I wasn't sure, but I decided to give it my best shot.

Even through the eighth grade, when some kids thought it wasn't cool, I always looked forward to show-and-tell. Not necessarily for myself, since I had very little to show and even less I wanted to tell. Listening to the other kids, however, gave me a snapshot of each one's personal life. Even though I felt pangs of jealousy at how carefree their lives seemed, I enjoyed seeing what they brought and tried my best to share in the experience of what made them happy or proud. It gave me an opportunity to see a side of someone that was usually left at home.

Whenever my turn arose, I usually talked about a new book I was reading. I got used to the giggling and dull stares that were reflected back at me.

*Sorry,* I thought to myself, *that's as good as it gets.*

But on one particular occasion I was lucky to have something very special to share with my disinterested classmates. I leaned down as I waited for my turn, double-checking my backpack. I fingered the smooth, 8-by-11-inch glossy photo, with which I was prepared to astonish them all. The night before, my father had walked into my bedroom as I was reading on my bed.

*Guess who came into the office today?* he asked.

*I don't know. Who?*

*Guess,* he coaxed with a smile.

*Um,* I tried to think of who it might have been. He seemed rather pleased, so it must have been someone he liked.

*Think about it,* he said impatiently. *We're in California. Think of someone famous.*

*Sylvester Stallone?* I ventured.

*No, dummy,* he snorted. *Mikhail Gorbachev!*

*But why did he come here?*

*I don't know. Jesus Christ, maybe he wanted to work on his tan.*

He walked over to me and whipped out a glossy photo of Mikhail Gorbachev. The inscription read:

*To Chip, a chip off the old block. Love from the Kremlin, Mikhail Gorbachev.*

After reading it, I looked back at my father. *Wow, he really did come here!*

*Sure he did. The proof is right there in your hands.*

I waited practically the entire hour for my turn, holding the photo tightly in my hands. Just when I thought I might never get called on, the teacher spoke my name. I walked eagerly to the front of the room and waited for everyone to quiet down. Once I was certain all eyes were upon me, I began.

"My parents manage an apartment building called International Towers. Sometimes, very important people come there to visit friends and relatives. Yesterday, my father was visited by a very, very important person."

Turning the picture around to face the class, I panned it slowly across the room.

"Mikhail Gorbachev. He autographed this picture and wrote the inscription to *me*," I added proudly.

"That's not real," someone blurted out.

"Yes, it is," I argued, drawing the photo back protectively.

"Why would *he* come to *your* house?" another kid laughed.

"I don't know. Maybe he was visiting someone," I said.

The class erupted into disarray. People were laughing and talking among themselves, sneaking glances at me. I stood there in disbelief, not knowing what to say. Thankfully, the brash sound of the bell ended the torture as everyone rushed toward the door.

"Chip?" the teacher asked.

I stood there staring at the floor.

"Chip, there must be some explanation. I don't believe you're lying. You're one of my straight-A students."

When I raised my head, I immediately realized it was a mistake. I could see the pity in her eyes behind the thin-framed glasses. Her mouth was frowning in empathy. I felt tears surfacing, but after years of practice I fought them back.

"I gotta go," I whispered. "I'm expected home soon."

Gathering my things as quickly as possible, I left the classroom, ran down the hall, and dashed out the door.

I tried to clear my mind, but I couldn't do it. The voices kept playing like a broken record—everyone laughing at me, mocking me. I couldn't wait to get home and lose myself in Robert Frost or Hemingway.

As I approached International Towers, I noticed something different. The address. The street address on the building read "700" in large gold numbers.

*She did it,* I thought.

My mother had convinced her boss that we could not live on the thirteenth floor, so eventually we packed up and moved to the twenty-eighth floor. Her next order of business was to change the building's address—666 East Ocean Boulevard. She explained that 666 was the unluckiest number of all and insisted on asking her boss to petition the city for a new street address. Obviously, she had succeeded.

I entered the apartment, hoping no one was home.

"Hey, bud," my father said.

"Oh, hi. What are you doing home?" I asked, disguising my disappointment.

"Uh, I'm playing hooker . . . er, I mean hooky," he whispered loudly. "What's the big hurry?" he asked.

"Oh, nothing. I just felt like reading for a while."

"All you do is read and write those stupid-ass poems," he said in a mocking tone. "Why don't you watch some TV with me for a change? You need some variety, ya know?"

After changing his clothes, he returned to the living room, settled down in his usual chair, and clicked on the television with the remote control. I took my place on the sofa as he switched channels, trying to find a program he liked. Bored, I glanced out the great picture window.

Although moving had been a hassle, we did gain an ocean view. I could see the *Queen Mary* docked at the marina, along with a huge white dome containing the wooden wonder— Howard Hughes's *Spruce Goose*. The beach was a bit drab and had hardly any waves because it had been carved into a slight inlet. As I watched boats cruise back and forth on the glistening water, I was suddenly jolted from my serenity.

"Chip, look!" my father said abruptly. "Look at her!"

Darting my head in the direction of the TV, I noticed a woman and a man talking. I searched for something unusual or strange about the woman, but found nothing.

"What is it?" I asked, baffled.

"Her! Isn't she hot?! Wow!" he said. "And look at that ass!" A huge smile spread across his face, and his eyes gleamed.

"I guess so," I said, disappointed.

By the way he was hollering, I had expected to see horns or a beard or something truly bizarre.

"No, she is hot," he said definitively. "Say she's hot."

"Why?"

"Say it. Say 'She's hot,'" he insisted.

"I don't know," I said uncomfortably.

"Chip, say it." His voice deepened to a serious tone.

"She's hot," I said flatly.

"There," he said, satisfied. "Yeah, she sure is."

We sat in silence for a while watching the show, until finally he spoke again.

"Hey, I have an idea," he said, turning off the TV.

"What?"

"You wanna scare Mom? She'll be home in a few minutes. How 'bout giving her a heart attack?" he laughed, jumping to his feet.

"What do you want to do?" I hesitated.

"Not me, champ. You!" He pointed at me with a sinister grin.

He shuffled to the glass door leading to the balcony. The latch gave a dull, metal, clicking sound as the door unlocked. With a hard pull, my father yanked open the sliding door and stepped outside.

"Come on, hurry! She'll be home any minute!" he said, waving me over.

"W-what do you want me to do?" I asked, feeling my blood turn cold.

"Get your ass out here and I'll show you! Don't make me ask you again!" he said viciously.

He waved impatiently while I crossed the room and stepped through the metal-framed doorway. Since we had moved to the new apartment, I had been on the balcony only a handful of times. While the view was amazing, my fear of heights usually confined me to the inside of the glass walls. As I stood there with my father, I became aware of the wind that whipped our clothes.

"Okay," he said, "now you climb over the railing and pretend like you're going to jump. I'll go inside and shut the door. When Mom comes home, she'll be scared shitless!"

"Dad, no!"

"Dad, no!" he mocked. "Oh, come on, quit being such a fucking pussy. Get your ass out there. I'll help you."

With his hand on my shoulder, he walked me over to the brown metal railing. I placed my hands on the cold frame and froze as the wind blew around us. Dark clouds were forming on the horizon. The boats that had been cutting back and forth across the water were returning to the dock for fear of being caught at sea in the building storm. The palm trees lining the beach swayed with the intensifying wind.

"Here," he said as he reached under my armpits to lift me over.

"No!" I cried. "I-I'll do it."

"Well, hurry up!"

The railing came up to about the center of my chest, so I needed to step between the vertical bars to boost myself up on the bottom railing. Wrapping both arms around the top of the railing, I lifted the rest of my body up, and then over.

I rested my feet on the outside of the bottom railing, locking the entire top half of my body down.

"Stand up!" he ordered.

He pried my body off the top railing, leaving only my hands to keep me from falling.

"There. Now when Mom comes home, just wait there until she

notices you. As soon as she does, pretend you're going to jump."

I wasn't paying attention to his instructions. I couldn't concentrate on anything but gluing my hands to the rail as the wind fought to disarm my grip.

I stared into my father's eyes, his hair blowing wildly as a puzzling smile appeared on his face. With a quick lunge, he pushed my shoulder forcefully.

"Dad! Dad, stop!" I screamed, fighting to keep my grip.

"Whoa! You scared?" he asked as he pushed me again.

"Yes! Please don't!"

"Okay," he said in a seemingly sympathetic voice.

"But how about this?" he asked, pounding a fist on my fingers.

My hands felt like ice. Had they not been so numb, his violent pounding probably would have hurt.

"Dad, please stop! I might fall!"

"Alright," he said, "I'll go back inside and wait for her. Remember, make it believable!"

I watched as he slammed the door shut and flipped the latch. I felt like a ghost, on the outside looking in. He sat at the dining room table and unfolded a newspaper. When he noticed me watching, he gave a thumbs-up.

I looked down to see where I'd land if I fell. Twenty-eight stories below was a small sidewalk leading to an outdoor parking lot. My hair obstructed my view as the wind flung it across my face. Behind me, dark clouds were rolling in to assault the city. My fingers were locked so tightly that my hands began to turn a stark white. I wondered what it would feel like to fall and hit the ground from this high up. All I had to do was let go. Just let go.

> *But that the dread of something after death—*
> *The undiscover'd country from whose bourn*
> *No traveler returns—puzzles the will*
> *And makes us rather bear those ills we have*

All I wanted to do was give up, but, like Hamlet, I was more afraid of dying than of living. I spotted motion out of the corner of my eye and watched intently as my mother entered the room. She placed her belongings on the kitchen counter and then glided over to kiss my father on the cheek. He looked up at her and said something that made her laugh. As she glanced up, our eyes met.

Her lips formed the word *Chip* in what appeared to be a scream.

She fumbled with the lock, trying desperately to open the glass door. I stared silently at her, tears frozen to my cheeks, as she leapt onto the balcony and grabbed my arms. With animal-like strength, she pulled me over the railing onto the safety of the balcony.

"My God, what happened?" she asked.

"It was just a game," I said quietly, placing my frigid hands under my shirt to warm them.

"That was great, Chip," he chimed in as we entered the living room.

"He wanted to scare you, Les. Shit, I wouldn't have gone out there. You got some guts, kid," he said, patting me on the back.

"Yeah," I said.

I didn't feel like I had guts. I was scared to death.

"Why don't you help me get the groceries out of the back of the car?" my mother asked me calmly. "I went shopping on my lunch hour and didn't have time to bring them up."

"Sure," I responded, eager to get out of my father's sight.

"Hurry up," my father snapped. "I'm hungry!"

"We'll be quick," she consoled as we closed the door to the apartment.

All the tenants' cars were parked in assigned spaces below the building in a multilevel, underground parking garage. It took some time traveling down the elevator, through the maze of concrete in the parking structure, to even reach the car. While unloading the bags from the trunk, my mother suddenly remembered something.

"Oh, shit, I forgot his dry cleaning," she said, exasperated.

Choosing between forgetting his clothes at the dry cleaner and being late for dinner was not a predicament I envied. My mother decided on the dry cleaners and told me to hang on as we peeled out of the parking space and through the garage. I waited in the car while she ran in to pick up the garments. Minutes later she emerged with a plastic bag holding my father's favorite pair of blue jeans—all pressed and starched. She hung them in the back of the car and then sped away.

Our arms were overloaded with plastic bags of groceries and dry cleaning, as we had to bring it all up to the apartment in only one trip. Once we made it through the parking garage to the elevator, we were home free. The doors opened, and we squeezed our way into the vertical trolley. When it reached our floor, we got off and walked down the circular hallway to our apartment.

"Hi, honey. W-what's wrong?" she said as she opened the door.

"You! You goddamn bitch! Where the hell have you been?! Do you have any idea what I've been going through?"

My father grabbed her by her clothes and pulled her into the room. I watched the turmoil unfold before me, the handles of the heavy grocery bags still cutting into my hands. He grabbed the bags she was holding and flung them across the room. I heard something that sounded like glass breaking. My father began punching her in the stomach and then in the face, screaming things I couldn't make out. Quietly lowering the bags to the ground, I tiptoed past the fight in the kitchen and on toward my bedroom.

"Sit down!" he screamed from behind.

I was so tired of the beatings, the yelling. Dropping to the sofa, I tried to distract myself by focusing on the TV, but it was no use. As I sat there, I began counting his swear words. So far, he had said some form of *fuck* twenty-one times, *cocksucker* four times, *bitch* twelve times, and *goddamn cunt* twice.

The couch I was sitting on had its back facing the kitchen, so I couldn't see what was happening. All of a sudden, something flew over my head and hit the glass door. A cereal box. My father began throwing things around the apartment. He ran past me to the sliding door and flung it open. To my amazement, he scooped up the cereal box and threw it over the balcony. He picked up other objects in the room—candles, coasters, a drinking glass—and fired them off in the same way. Then, with an unearthly yell, he grabbed a metal TV tray and crushed it in his hands as if it were a piece of paper.

My mother ran over to stop him. "Dave, don't!"

"Shut up!" he said, as he slammed her down onto the couch next to me and resumed hitting her. I brought my legs to my chest in an effort to protect myself.

"Do you want me to tell him what happened to him when he was three? Do you?" he asked wildly.

"No," she whimpered. "He's too young!"

"I'm gonna kill you! Ahhh!" he screamed as he grabbed for her throat.

At that moment something in me snapped. I wanted out.

Working on pure instinct, I barreled toward the front door. I hurdled over the grocery bags, swung open the door, and ran out into the hallway. Not wanting to wait for the elevator, I dashed into the stairwell. The echo of my footsteps bounding down flight after flight of stairs was interrupted by a voice.

"Chip, get back here!" my mother yelled.

But I wasn't stopping. I didn't ever want to go back there again.

*I'd rather die,* I thought.

Emerging in the lobby, I searched frantically for the security guard, but he was nowhere to be found. I stood there in the cold, desolate hall, shaking uncontrollably. A minute later my mother stepped out of the elevator and stomped toward me. Her face was bruised and stressed, a flicker of hate in her eyes.

"Get your fucking little ass back up there!"

"No, Mom, let's leave! Let's get out of here!"

"Tough shit. We're both in this for the long haul."

"I won't! I—"

She dug her fingernails into my arm as she glared at me viciously.

"You *will* get back up there, you little bastard! This is *it*. *This* is life. There's no turning back, no escape. You can do it the easy way or the hard way," she said, her nails pressing deeper into my flesh.

In that moment, something in me changed. I knew she was right: There was no escaping. My mother made that very clear. With that, a numbness washed over me, a feeling of detachment. Whatever life was going to throw my way, I was just going to have to deal with it. I had no options, no choices. Hopes and dreams were something other people wrote about in books. They were not my reality. My reality was violence, hatred, and fear. Life, I decided, was not about living, but about surviving.

# CHAPTER
# 7

# Prelude to a Dream

AFTER A COUPLE OF years, my parents decided to move back to Michigan," I explained, averting my eyes to the table at which I was seated.

The pain in retelling the hell I called a childhood was taking its toll on me. I fingered the glossy photo of Mikhail Gorbachev that my father told me had been personally autographed by the Soviet leader.

"My father either lost or quit his job at International Towers. My mother continued to work there for about six months, while my father found another complex to manage. Soon after, we packed up and returned to Michigan. But not before a month-long stay with my Aunt Chris and Uncle Mark in Indiana."

"Aunt Chris," repeated one of the board members. "That would be Christine Clark, your father's sister. Are you aware that she has offered to open her home to him should we grant parole?"

"That's her decision to make," I stated.

"Okay. Please continue."

"We moved to a city a bit south of where we used to live. That is where I eventually attended high school, and where," I paused and smiled to myself, my heart feeling a little lighter as I prepared to speak her name, "I met Lisa."

My eyes opened to a darkened room. The house was still and quiet in the dead of night as I silently slipped out of bed and groped for the light switch. Squinting to filter the onslaught of light, I frantically searched for a pencil and paper. I had awakened from the most vivid, wonderful dream of my life and needed to write down the details before I forgot them. I jotted down notes, trying in vain to recapture the feelings and sensations of the dream.

*I was on a lonely, rolling ship at sea, sailing for what seemed to be weeks, searching for land but finding not a trace. Below deck, I peered out through a great bay door that sat level with the ocean. As I stood there, a dolphin sailed into the air and then plunged back into the shimmering brilliance. I waited anxiously for it to come back. The sea laid as calm as a sheet of glass while the bright morning sun graced its surface.*

*With a loud rush of water, the dolphin propelled itself into the air again, then splashed back down, each time coming closer to my ship. With a final leap, the beautiful creature lunged into the opening where I was standing. I quickly stepped aside.*

*To my amazement, upon touching the surface of my ship, the dolphin changed shape. Now kneeling before me, it had become a young woman with flowing dark hair and eyes the color of the sea. I was speechless. The graceful figure came to me and took my hands. Her face reflected such purity and beauty that my heart cried out and I longed to hold her. As her head tilted, she pressed her lips to mine, leaving me breathless, enraptured, and complete.*

In the predawn darkness, I fought desperately to cling to the breathless sense of wonder I was feeling. If only I could feel that connection and love, not only in a dream, but in real life.

Sinking down onto my bed, I turned to study the oil painting I had finished days before of a winding stream under a gray, cloudy sky. Although the grass and trees in the foreground lacked dimension, the landscape appeared foreboding, almost dreadful. Dawn was breaking. Soon it would be time to leave for school, so I threw on some clothes and studied myself in the mirror. Black leather jacket, black T-shirt, and black jeans to match my mood.

"Just a tad morbid," I said aloud.

I went to my closet and rifled through the hanging clothes for a new shirt, suddenly remembering something my friend Tom had said to me.

*Do you smoke? Man, your clothes smell like smoke.*

Leaving my bedroom, I spotted a light in the kitchen. My mother was already awake.

"Mom?"

"Yeah, what?" she answered from another room.

"Tom said my clothes all smell like smoke. You guys smoke so much that people think I do."

"Just a minute," she sighed.

I had a white-and-blue striped shirt almost off a hanger when my mother returned, whipping a can of Glade air freshener out from behind her back. Before I could stop her, she was dousing all of the clothes in my closet with the entire contents of the can. Grabbing the shirt I was about to put on, she doused it as well.

"Are you kidding?"

"At least it won't smell like smoke!"

Having no better alternative, I put the new shirt on and tried to mask the scent with cologne. Now smelling like Glade and cologne, I decided to go outside and air myself out while waiting for my father to drive me to school.

"Hey, are you going to shave? You look like a goddamn bum," he said, approaching the car and motioning for me to get in.

I raised my hand to my chin and felt a bit of stubble.

"No, not today. It's not too bad," I replied as I clicked my seat belt.

"The hell it ain't! And look at your hair. You look like a greasy Mexican."

"Yeah," I said, turning toward the window.

He kept talking on our way to the high school, and I must have been deep in thought because he put his hand on my knee and shook it roughly.

"Ya know?" he said loudly.

"Huh?" I asked, startled.

"I said," he began with a sigh, "the guy ended up getting life in prison. It was a bum rap, ya know?"

"Oh, yeah," I agreed, not knowing what I had agreed to.

"Prison would be tough, wouldn't it?" he asked.

"Sure. I'd never want to go there."

"What would you do if you found out I'd been to prison?" he asked as we pulled into the unloading zone in front of the school.

"You? In prison?" He seemed too neat and orderly. "For what?" I asked, not quite sure where he was going with this discussion.

"Bank robbery. Hell, I don't know. What would you do?" he pressed.

"I don't know. As long as I'm not a bank, I suppose there's nothing to worry about," I said dully, reaching for the door handle.

"Yeah, right," he laughed.

⌾══✦══⌾

"That's very good, Chip. Very lifelike," Ms. Beasley whispered from behind me.

"Thanks," I responded, studying her through the standing mirror in the front of the art classroom.

My reflection stared back at me with cold, vacant eyes. Charcoal in hand, I stroked vigorously, trying to capture my likeness on paper. I rubbed my blackened finger across the bluish-gray paper, transforming two-dimensional shapes into a human cheekbone, an eye with a lifeless stare.

"Self-portraits," she began, bending down to meet my reflection, "can be frustrating for some people. You seem to be doing just fine, though."

I smiled at her as she glanced from my reflection to the paper several times.

"You have a scar on your forehead," she said in a concerned voice.

"Yeah," I began running my finger along the half-inch-long, narrow wound. "My mom said I was in the backseat of my grandmother's car when I was about three years old. My grandmother apparently made a quick turn and I fell onto the floor of the car, cutting my head on the lid of an oil can."

"Really?" she said incredulously.

"That's what she said."

"Well, you're still a good-looking guy!" She smiled and pinched my cheek.

Of all the classes during my junior year of high school, I enjoyed art the most—next to English literature of course.

# READER/CUSTOMER CARE SURVEY

We care about your opinions! Please take a moment to fill out our online Reader Survey at **http://survey.hcibooks.com**.
As a **"THANK YOU"** you will receive a **VALUABLE INSTANT COUPON** towards future book purchases as well as a **SPECIAL GIFT** available only online! Or, you may mail this card back to us and we will send you a copy of our exciting catalog with your valuable coupon inside.
(PLEASE PRINT IN ALL CAPS)

First Name _____ MI. _____ Last Name _____

Address _____

State _____ Zip _____ Email _____ City _____

**1. Gender**
☐ Female ☐ Male

**2. Age**
☐ 8 or younger
☐ 9-12 ☐ 13-16
☐ 17-20 ☐ 21-30
☐ 31+

**3. Did you receive this book as a gift?**
☐ Yes ☐ No

**4. Annual Household Income**
☐ under $25,000
☐ $25,000 - $34,999
☐ $35,000 - $49,999
☐ $50,000 - $74,999
☐ over $75,000

**5. What are the ages of the children living in your house?**
☐ 0 - 14 ☐ 15+

**6. Marital Status**
☐ Single
☐ Married
☐ Divorced
☐ Widowed

**7. How did you find out about the book?**
*(please choose one)*
☐ Recommendation
☐ Store Display
☐ Online
☐ Catalog/Mailing
☐ Interview/Review

**8. Where do you usually buy books?**
*(please choose one)*
☐ Bookstore
☐ Online
☐ Book Club/Mail Order
☐ Price Club (Sam's Club, Costco's, etc.)
☐ Retail Store (Target, Wal-Mart, etc.)

**9. What subject do you enjoy reading about the most?**
*(please choose one)*
☐ Parenting/Family
☐ Relationships
☐ Recovery/Addictions
☐ Health/Nutrition
☐ Christianity
☐ Spirituality/Inspiration
☐ Business Self-help
☐ Women's Issues
☐ Sports

**10. What attracts you most to a book?**
*(please choose one)*
☐ Title
☐ Cover Design
☐ Author
☐ Content

TAPE IN MIDDLE; DO NOT STAPLE

FOLD HERE

**Comments**

When it came time for my English literature class each day, I could think of nothing else. The class studied, in great depth, some of the finest literary works of all time. Most of them I had already read, but there were a few I hadn't. I had been studying various works by Plato when our teacher asked us to write an essay on any book we chose. Without much thought, I chose *The Republic* by Plato.

*Are you sure you can write a proper essay on that book?* my teacher asked.

*Yes, I've already read quite a bit of it. I feel I can write a very good essay.*

*Go for it, then.*

There I sat, anxiously awaiting my grade on the essay. English literature was my last class of the day, so it was almost nauseating anticipating the results. I had spent the better part of three weeks actually reading the book, and only a couple of days writing the essay. Perhaps I was a little rusty, and I might not have conveyed my thoughts clearly. Maybe the grammar left something to be desired. There was only one way to find out. The moment the teacher called me to the front of the class to pick up my essay, I studied his expression for any sign of my grade.

His face and eyes were hard as stone as he handed my essay back to me, upside down. Before he let go of it, he smiled.

"A fine job."

A large **A** in bright red ink jumped out when I flipped it over. With a sigh of relief, I read through the corrections in grammar and the constructive comments. Then I took my seat proudly and placed the paper into my bookbag.

Later that evening, I tried to share my essay with my father.

"Dad, are you listening?"

"I'm listening!" my father moaned, rolling his eyes.

I attempted for the third time. The other two were interrupted by the flipping of channels on the television, followed by uncontrollable coughing spells.

I stumbled over a few of the words as I tried to race through the paper before there was another interruption.

"Hi, Rocky!" my father shouted upon the entrance of our family poodle.

I ignored him and kept reading.

"Boogy, woogy, woogy! How's Wocky doing?" he continued as he picked up the dog.

I stopped and stared at him.

"Okay," he laughed. "I'll stop. We'll both listen. Listen to Chip, Rocky."

"No, it's okay. It's just a dumb essay."

"I *said* we'll listen. Now read it."

I continued where I had left off, but within seconds I was stopped again.

"Rocky farted! It wasn't me."

"Come on, Dad."

"Okay, okay. I promise, I won't interrupt you again."

As I opened my mouth to continue, my father resumed making loud, unintelligible noises.

"Beep boop bloop!" he shouted.

"Forget it," I said. As I left the room, I heard an eruption of laughter.

When my mother arrived home from work, I eagerly greeted her with essay in hand.

"Good job," she said, opening a can of pasta sauce.

"Would *you* like to hear it?"

"Sure, but I'm gonna make dinner while you read."

I finally succeeded in reading it from beginning to end, uninterrupted. Well aware that my mother may not have been paying attention—she was juggling several pots and pans in an effort to prepare dinner—I still felt a sense of contentment at having read the whole thing to someone.

When I was finished, I retired the paper to the counter.

"Mom, why do I have this scar?" I asked, pointing to my forehead.

"Huh, I don't know. Did you bump it?" she asked as she placed a bowl of steaming spaghetti on the kitchen table.

"You told me I had fallen in the backseat of Grandma's car and cut myself on an oil can."

"Oh, maybe that's what happened."

"But you're the one who told me."

"Chip, I have to get dinner ready. Would you leave me alone until then?"

During dinner, silence filled the air except for the sounds of our forks clinking against the plates. At last, the stillness was broken by my father.

"You wanna go watch some TV?"

"Sure."

As we all settled down in the living room, I gazed out the window, waiting for the program to begin.

"I forgot my sleeping pills. Would you get them for me?" my father asked.

"Sure," I said, getting up to find his insomnia pills.

I found them in their usual place in the cupboard. After removing the little blue pills from their foil package, I discarded the empty box into the garbage.

"That was the last of them," I began. "You're going to have to . . . hey!"

At the last second, I noticed what the empty box of pills was resting on. Right there in the garbage, alongside banana peels, soup cans, and dirty paper towels, was my essay.

"You threw it away!" I hollered.

"What?" my mother inquired casually.

"My essay! It's in the garbage!"

I bent down and retrieved it, brushing the grime from its surface.

"Oh, sorry."

"That was really important to me."

"She said she was sorry," my father growled, glaring. "Now sit down."

*Was it really an accident, or did she think it was garbage after hearing it? Maybe that's why my teacher seemed reluctant to approve my essay choice; maybe he gave me an A only because he felt sorry for me. Maybe I was just fooling myself.*

Without another word, I handed my father his pills and resumed my seat on the sofa. Before long, my eyes shifted back to the last of the autumn leaves outside, just barely visible in the dusky light.

A few weeks later, Christmas was upon us.

The harsh glare of headlights caused me to avert my eyes from the wet, slushy road to the soft, white snow underfoot. I moved with an easy rhythm through the light, pale dust as I traced my way along the sidewalk. The sun had long since set, and with darkness came a cold, bitter wind that forced its way through the openings in my clothing. I rested my hands inside the pockets of my black leather jacket and folded the collar up around my neck. The streets were practically empty, as could be expected on Christmas Day.

I needed time to think. I was very confused—about myself, about life, about everything. I didn't want to go home because I was sick to the deepest pit of my soul—sick of the chaos and unpredictability, sick of the violence and pain. I searched for glimmers of hope, but found none.

I had a few friends, but the relationships were shallow at best. It was becoming unbearable for me to force small talk about video games, sports, or music when I had so much on my mind. Perhaps no one cared anyway, and I was afraid of what they would think of me if they found out. Perhaps they were battling their own demons. Unable to open up to anyone and uncertain about where to turn, I felt terribly lonely and distraught.

As I reached the sidewalk leading to my house, I came to a halt. The large front window allowed a clear view into the brightly lit living room. My father was sitting in his usual chair, cigarette in hand, eyes focused on the television. My mother was passing through with an armload of clothes on her way to the laundry room.

My father reminded me on a number of occasions that my mother's drinking problem was my fault. I also deduced that I was responsible for the violence at home, since after the beatings my mother would turn away from me, dodging my embraces and attempts to comfort her. Maybe I was too much of a coward to protect her. At any rate, my father was always disappointed in me. I often heard him say how much he hated me, that I was stupid and worthless. *You little son of a bitch! You'll never be a man! You're no son of mine. . . . I wish I never laid eyes on you, Jack!*

I stood outside looking into not only my house, but also my life. It was like a bitter pill that I choked down every day, hoping it would get easier to swallow. And, in the end, after all the suffering and hurt, for what? The ends didn't seem to justify the means. Suddenly, I knew what I had to do, and a sense of calmness and quiet determination suffused my soul.

"What do you mean you're sick?" my mother snapped.

"My throat is pretty sore. I probably shouldn't have walked home in the cold."

"No shit," she agreed as she walked out of my bedroom. "I can't believe you're going to miss the first day back to school."

"I'm sorry."

The sound of the front door shutting told me I was alone in the house. I slowly crept out of bed and peered through the living room window. My mother's car sped away in a cloud of exhaust as she headed for work. My father left early and came home late, so for at least the next eight hours I would have the privacy to do what needed to be done.

As I walked through the house on my way to the kitchen, I realized that everything I was touching, everything I was looking at, would be for the last time. I entered the kitchen, reached for an ice-cold can of Pepsi from the refrigerator, and opened it with a crack. While rummaging through the cabinet, grave decisions invited my hand to select my *coup de grace*—a bottle of sleeping pills. I was in luck; it felt almost full. After shaking most of the small white pills into my hand, I replaced the lid and returned the bottle to the shelf, adjusting the direction of the label to prevent the immediate detection of what I was soon to do. I gazed out the window, sleeping pills in one hand, Pepsi in the other, and studied the overcast sky. I wondered if I would go to heaven or hell.

*Anywhere would be better than this.*

In case cowardice overcame my resolve, I crammed as many of the pills as I could into my mouth, leaving only a small opening for the Pepsi to swish them down my throat. After several gulps of soda, I clanged the can onto the counter and walked toward my bedroom to die.

When I closed my door, the room became a moonless midnight. I felt my way over to the CD player and selected the music I wanted to hear while I drifted into eternal sleep. The slow, soft piano began and would continue to play until I was discovered, for I had placed the song on repeat mode. Beethoven's *Moonlight Sonata* reached to the very core of my being. It seemed to differ so from other music, much as poetry differs from a simple story. To me, poetry was like music for the eyes, while classical music was poetry for the ears.

As the melancholy song played on, I thought of the genius of Beethoven, Mozart, Chopin, and Vivaldi. Their lives had meaning, truth, and purpose. Their emotions sang clearly through their music, as did Emerson's, Whitman's, Shakespeare's, and Burns's through their written word. They impacted the world with their feelings. I knew I could never achieve such greatness because my mind was full of despair, fear, confusion, frustration, bitterness, anxiety, and denial. I had put up my walls, fastened my restraints, and tried to tackle all life had to offer. Even so, my contribution to the world was misery. All those around me seemed infected by my presence.

"To be or not to be, that is the question," I said aloud, crawling beneath the covers of my bed.

"Not to be," I shuddered.

An annoying ringing dragged me from the deepest slumber I had ever experienced. *Ring. Ring. Ring.* My brain told my body to move, but my arms were not responding correctly. The last thing I remembered was lying in my bed, attempting to fall asleep. I had been fighting the urge to leap out of bed and force myself to vomit, until at last the sleeping pills took effect. *Ring. Ring. Ring.* My mind was cloudy as I struggled to get up. There seemed to be a definite lack of communication between my brain and the body attached to it. My legs wobbled awkwardly as I staggered out of my room toward the kitchen. I used my hands to steady the room as I walked, for it lurched up and spun wildly before my eyes. After quite an effort, I reached the ringing phone and lifted the handset.

"'Lo?" I managed to mumble.

"Chip, what's wrong?" my mother asked. "Are you drunk?"

"No. T-took . . . pills," I stammered.

"What? Why?"

"Kill . . . myse-myself."

"Goddamn you! Wait right there. I'm coming home!"

Feeling as if I might lose consciousness, I dropped the handset and plopped down into a chair at the kitchen table, resting my head on my arms. I was too tired to think. After what seemed an eternity, my mother burst through the door.

"Come on," she yelled. "We're going to the hospital! I'm so disappointed in you!"

"Sorry," I whispered as she walked me to the door.

Under the blinding lights in the emergency room, my head fell back and forth as I faded in and out of consciousness.

"Drink this," a stocky nurse instructed, handing me a small paper cup filled with thick, black liquid. "It's liquid charcoal. It will help you vomit. If you don't vomit, we'll have to pump your stomach. We're waiting for the x-rays right now. As soon as you drink that, drink this one."

She produced another paper cup with what looked like chocolate milk.

"This will get rid of the taste of the charcoal."

Sniffing the thick liquid, I downed it in a single gulp and then moved on to the chocolate milk.

"You did that like a pro," she sneered. "You must be used to this."

I didn't have the strength to respond to her, but I figured that when it was time to vomit, I would make sure it was in her direction.

I was sitting on the emergency room bed when the curtain was drawn back, revealing a doctor.

"Hi, Chip. How do you feel?" he asked nicely.

"Okay."

"Well, unfortunately the pills have already been digested. There will be no need to pump your stomach, but I'm really concerned about your liver. How many pills do you suppose you ingested?"

"At . . . least th-thirty."

"We're going to have to do a few more tests. You may have permanently damaged your liver with that level of medication."

I nodded.

"Just relax. Here. Vomit into this when you feel like you have to," he said, before vanishing behind the curtain.

Almost immediately after he left, I jolted forward, throwing up uncontrollably. I tried to aim for the receptacle he had handed me, but I was getting more on the floor than in the pan. Without a word, the nurse returned and bent down to clean up the mess.

Exhausted, I slumped into the bed and exhaled a sigh of relief.

"Sorry," I said, turning to the nurse.

Before she could respond, the curtain was forcefully thrown back, exposing my father's burning glare.

"Look what you've done," he began coldly. "How *dare* you do this to me!"

"I-I," I stammered.

"I don't even want to talk to you. I can't believe you. You really let me down, Chip. You really let me down," he said, shaking his head.

"No visitors. He needs his rest," interjected the nurse as she crossed the room and drew the curtain, closing my father out. Before leaving, she looked at me, pity resting in her eyes. With an awkward smile she departed, closing the curtain behind her.

I even failed at suicide. Now I had no idea what to do. Shakespeare had written of tomorrow in *Macbeth*:

*Tomorrow, and tomorrow, and tomorrow,*
*Creeps in this petty pace from day to day,*
*To the last syllable of recorded time;*
*And all our yesterdays have lighted fools*
*The way to dusty death.*

*Slowly*, I supposed, *the future continues to move on, from one day to the next, into forever.*

# CHAPTER
# 8

# Dawn of Tomorrow

AFTER MY SUICIDE ATTEMPT, I lived one day at a time. If one day provided no answers, no sign of relief, perhaps another would.

On one of my first days back to school as a senior, I was climbing a flight of stairs, trying to avoid the oncoming traffic of students scurrying to class. As I looked up to the landing above, I saw familiar sea-blue eyes staring directly into mine. She had long, dark hair that seemed to flow like cascading water when she walked. Her eyes glittered like sunlight off a serene lake. I stood dumbfounded as she came toward me, a slight smile on her lips. As mysterious winged creatures engaged in battle inside my stomach, a cold wave swept over me—she was the girl from my dream.

"Hey, Chip!" Tom called from behind her.

Letting her long hair fall across her face, she lowered her head and quickly rushed past me, down the stairs and out of sight.

"What?" I asked, meeting him with a handshake on the stairs.

"Come on, I have to tell you something," he smiled as he walked me to my locker. "She asked about you."

"Who?" I asked, although in my heart I knew who he meant.

"That girl with the long hair."

"What did she say?"

"She asked who you were. What your name was."

"What did you say?"

"I said your name was Chip. What did you think I was going to say? Her locker is right over there," he said, pointing across the hallway.

"Thanks," I said as the bell sounded. "I'll try to talk to her after class."

"Good luck!" he said, patting me on the back.

*If fate will have it meant to be, then it was meant to be,* I thought, as I walked to my next class.

John James Ingalls once wrote of fate and opportunity:

> *Mortals desire, and conquer every foe*
> *Save death; but those who doubt or hesitate,*
> *Condemned to failure, penury and woe,*
> *Seek me in vain and uselessly implore—*
> *I answer not, and I return no more.*

I wondered if John James Ingalls had ever been seventeen.

Time seemed to stand still that hour, and as soon as class was over, I bolted back to the hall where fate awaited me at the ring of the bell. Pretending to be doing something important in my locker, I anxiously waited for her to show up. I turned over different things to say in my mind. I didn't know if I should be direct, debonair, sophisticated, funny, or cool. Of course, my mind went blank as I watched her approach her locker and spin the dial on the combination lock.

*It's now or never,* I thought, crossing the hall and walking up beside her.

When she noticed me, her face lit up with the most beautiful smile. Knowing I should say something, I spoke the first words that entered my mind.

"I heard you were asking about me," I pointed out playfully, trying to maintain my best James Dean composure by leaning against the lockers.

"Yeah, I asked your friend what your name was," she laughed.

"It's Chip."

"I know."

"What's your name?"

"Lisa."

"Lisa, huh? Would you like to go out sometime? I mean, can I have your phone number?"

"Sure." She smiled as she found a piece of paper to write on.

"What about *your* number?" she asked.

"Oh, here," I said as I took the pen from her and wrote my

own phone number down. "Okay, well . . . it was nice talking to you."

"Yeah, it was nice talking to you, too. Bye," she said, pushing her locker shut with a soft click.

As she walked away, I knew my life had changed forever. Even after our brief talk, I was feeling emotions I had never felt before, emotions that I never even knew existed.

The dawn of the tomorrow for which I had been patiently waiting had come, and the two weeks that followed were the most exhilarating of my life. Lisa and I talked on the phone practically every day. I had never met anyone so deep, so open. My thoughts were completely consumed by her. When she greeted me at school, my heart lightened instantly. Lisa was understanding and patient and seemed to value my mind. Being near her just felt right. When we talked, it was as if I was chatting with an old, familiar friend; there were no pretenses, no discontent. For the first time in my life, everything felt perfect and right—until my parents wanted to meet her.

Throughout my life, I avoided bringing friends back to my house as much as possible. I didn't want an embarrassing outburst by my father to destroy a friendship. But my parents had been wondering who was occupying all my time, and my father thought it would be a good idea to invite Lisa over to dinner so they could meet her. Realizing that I couldn't put off this meeting forever, I reluctantly agreed. I prepared Lisa by describing my father's military history. I let her know that sometimes he could get a little strange due to post-traumatic stress disorder.

Surprisingly, Lisa told me that her father had been in Vietnam, too. At least my father and Lisa would have something to talk about.

As I finished washing my face, I glanced at my watch. Lisa would be arriving in roughly twenty minutes. My face dripping, I groped through squinted eyes for a towel. The cold metal of the bar told me that the towels must have been removed for washing. I began to hunt for a spare as the water turned cold on my face. After a thorough search in the bathroom, I walked into the hall to check the linen closet.

"Can I help you, Chip?" my mother asked impatiently.

"I need a towel to dry my face."

"Well, you know better than that. You ask *me* if you need a towel."

She handed over a small, cream-colored cotton towel, which I eagerly used to dry my face and hands. Those were the rules of the house. For as long as I could remember, I was not permitted to look through drawers, cupboards, or closets. Not even for a bath towel.

"Ugh," I moaned as I smelled the linen cloth. "It reeks of smoke. Mom, can you guys try not to smoke when Lisa gets here?"

"Alright."

"And could you tell Dad not to swear all the time?"

"You tell him yourself," she said coldly.

Knowing that was not an option, I shook my head.

"Just try to keep him calm, then. Could you also try not to drink so much beer?"

"Jesus Christ, okay, okay!" she snapped as she turned to leave. "Anything else?"

Given past experience, I knew it was futile to expect anything better than what was bound to happen. I just had to hope for the best.

"This lasagna is wonderful," Lisa commented with a smile to my mother.

"Thank you, hon. I have chocolate cake for dessert."

Though the evening was uneventful, my stomach was in knots as I watched my father for any sign of a storm brewing. I thought it would be a good idea if I could get Lisa and him to talk about something.

"Lisa's father was in Vietnam, too."

"Oh, really?" my father said, sitting back in his chair. "Which branch of the service was he in?"

"The navy," she began. "He was stationed in Saigon, working in an office building."

"Did he see any action?"

"Well, not like you did. Chip told me about what you went through."

"Yeah," my father nodded as he rolled a toothpick from one corner of his mouth to the other. "I went to the jungles three times. Got shot three times, too. My first tour over there, boy was I green. They shot me right in the head."

"What!" Lisa exclaimed.

"You can feel the dent. Come here and feel it."

"Dave, not at the dinner table," my mother objected.

"It's not like my fucking brains are gonna come pouring out all of a sudden. The wound healed after almost thirty years!"

Lisa got up and walked to my father's side. He grabbed her hand and placed her finger on the dent I had felt many times before.

"Oh my gosh!" she gasped.

"Boy, she smells nice. Doesn't she, Chip?"

"Yeah," I answered, my eyes fixed on my plate.

While Lisa returned to her seat, my father continued.

"I spilled a lot of blood over there. My own . . . and others'."

"You had to kill people?" Lisa gulped.

"Sure, that's what war's about."

"H-how many?" she stammered.

I reached out my foot from under the table and nudged Lisa. As she turned to look at me, she put her head down.

"Sorry, I shouldn't have asked that."

"No, no," my father said, realizing what I had done. "Chip, if you can't stand the heat, stay out of the kitchen. Lisa and I want to talk."

"Come on, Chip. Help me get the cake," my mother prodded.

I cleared the table of dishes while my father relayed stories about Vietnam.

". . . so the final count is unclear. Officially, it's seventy-five confirmed kills. When I was captured, though, I probably killed twice that many to escape."

"You were captured?" Lisa asked sympathetically.

"Yep, for six months . . ."

They kept talking while I sliced the cake and helped my mother clean up. When she reached for a can of beer, I glared at her.

"Oh, shit! Lisa doesn't care if I have a beer, do you, Lisa?"

"What? Oh, no, go ahead."

"See, dick-nose," my mother said as she stuck out her tongue. When I didn't react, she swung a fist into my upper arm. Not just a normal fist, but the kind with the knuckle of the middle finger raised to ensure extra pain.

"Ow! Come on, Mom."

"I was just teasing," she giggled.

"Don't be a pussy, Chip," my father added. "And don't interrupt. I was telling Lisa about how I got zippered by the gooks in '63."

He leaned back to lift up his sweatshirt. Watching her face intently, he slowly revealed the long white scar on his abdomen.

"Wow!" she gasped.

"This is where the sons-of-bitches got me. Of course, I wasn't so fat then."

"You're not fat, honey," my mother interjected.

"What is it then—muscle?" he snorted as he pulled his shirt back down.

"Yep," she said, polishing off the rest of the beer.

For the remainder of the evening, I tried to steer the conversation to simple, uncomplicated issues. The sound of a car pulling up in the driveway rained a shower of relief over me.

"Your dad is here, Lisa," I said.

"Okay. Well, it was nice meeting you."

Lisa stood up and walked to the door. My parents bid her farewell as I walked her outside to the car.

"Hello," I greeted her father.

"Hi," he smiled back.

I had met Lisa's father for the first time only a few days before. I didn't quite know where I stood with him. He didn't say much to me when Lisa had introduced us, and I didn't think he liked me very much. His silent demeanor made me a little uneasy. I thought of him as a cat, ready to lunge at any moment. So, not wanting to get lunged at, I quickly hugged Lisa goodbye and ran back into my house.

I found my mother in the kitchen wrapping up the leftover cake and placing it in the refrigerator. My father was sitting at the table doing a crossword puzzle.

"Well, what do you think?" I asked them.

"She's a real piece of work," my father said, shaking his head as he removed his eyeglasses.

"What do you mean?" I asked.

"She's very manipulative. Trust me, she's on her best behavior now. Her true colors will come through soon enough."

"But I thought you liked her . . . her father. You guys talked about Vietnam and—"

"She was trying to get on my good side. Didn't you see her fake expressions? 'Oh, this lasagna is wonderful,'" he mocked.

"_I_ thought she was genuine," I argued.

"Okay, believe what you want. You're not gonna to listen to me. But, remember, I warned you. Jesus, her father didn't see any action. He was a pussy. I was the one out there defending our country, spilling my guts in the jungles, so he could sit his lazy ass in an office."

"Chip, why don't you let Dad work his crossword. Go watch some TV or something," injected my mother.

"Hey, Chip," he called after me. "Just to show you that I know what I'm talking about, I'll bet you a hundred bucks she'll call you tonight and tell you to thank us for our hospitality just to get on our good side. Mark my words."

I closed my bedroom door and stretched out onto my bed, staring up at the ceiling. Why hadn't I seen Lisa as manipulative? Was my father right? I wondered how he could read her so well, when I thought I knew her better than he did. Was I lovestruck and blind?

As I lay there with conflicting thoughts swirling around my mind, the phone rang.

# CHAPTER
## 9

# Poison of Doubt

ONCE ACCEPTED, THE DROP of poison my father offered me about Lisa took hold in my mind and threatened to kill the bond between us. Occasionally, he would make predictions about her, and he was usually, undeniably correct.

*Tell her you wanna see some of your other friends,* he would say. *Avoid her phone calls and watch her get upset.*

So I would do it.

"But we had plans to go out," Lisa argued.

"My dad said you would get like this," I snorted. "You don't want me to have any friends."

"Yes, I do. But we had plans. Can't you see your friends another night?"

"I suppose so," I conceded, seeing how hurt she was.

Later that evening my father confronted me.

"So you went out with her again, huh? Boy, she's got you whipped."

"It's not like that, Dad. I made a promise to go out with her tonight. I can see them some other time. Besides, you complain even when I hang out with my other friends."

"Don't be a smart-ass! I'll knock you on your ass, punk!"

"Okay, okay. I'm sorry, it's just that I'd rather—"

"You would rather be a fucking wimp. Man, you've changed, Chip. I'm really disappointed."

I began ignoring Lisa's calls in an effort to make my father happy.

*That's my boy,* he'd say proudly. *Don't let her get her hooks in you. Let's watch a movie together.*

And on it would go. I wrestled with doubt, that great invisible adversary I had allowed to slowly creep into my dreams and steal them away. I could see what my father was saying, but Lisa was so sincere and kind that his predictions didn't completely make sense. I was torn. I began to resent them both for placing me in such a predicament.

Attempting to make peace, Lisa decided to call my father at work. When he arrived home that evening, he told me about their conversation.

"Lisa called me today," he said, removing his overcoat and setting down his briefcase with a thud on the dull linoleum kitchen floor.

"She did?" I asked, feeling relieved that the tension might soon be over.

"Uh-huh. She asked if Mr. David Michael St. Clair was there."

"She asked like that?"

"Exactly. She tried to control the whole conversation; some bullshit about making herself part of the family. She's got a lot of balls."

I couldn't believe my ears. I had heard enough. When she called later that evening, I was ready to give her a piece of my mind.

"Hi," Lisa beamed as I answered the phone.

"What do you want?" I asked in an icy tone.

"What's wrong? Didn't your dad tell you I called him today?"

"Sure he did. You asked for Mr. David Michael St. Clair. He said you commanded the whole conversation."

"What! Th-that's not true!" she cried in disbelief. "We had a very nice conversation. I never asked for him like that. I was scared to death to talk to him, but he was so open and sympathetic. He seemed so happy when we hung up."

"Are you calling my father a liar?" I demanded.

"I swear it didn't happen that way! Chip, I didn't even know that was your dad's middle name," her voice faded into tears.

*Maybe there had been a misunderstanding,* I thought.

As my senior year came to a close and I began applying to colleges, my father became even moodier, snapping at my mother and me constantly. One day, when I was in my room talking on the phone with Lisa, he exploded like a ton of dynamite.

"What was that sound?" Lisa asked suddenly.

"It sounds like my father's hitting my mother! Hold on!"

I threw down the receiver and ran into the family room. My mother was cowering on the sofa, shielding her head from his powerful blows. When he spotted me, he charged like a bull. I stood paralyzed with fear as he grabbed me and threw me into my bedroom.

"Stay the fuck out of my way!" he growled as he slammed the door shut.

"Lisa, I gotta go! I'm calling the police!"

Without waiting for a response, I hung up and dialed 911.

Voice quivering, I explained that my father was beating my mother. I told the dispatcher that my father was an ex–Green Beret who made it crystal clear he knew how to kill people. The voice on the other end asked me question after question for what seemed like a lifetime. Finally the police arrived at our front door with a bellowing knock.

I ran to my bedroom door and swung it open. My father was leading two uniformed officers into the house, while my mother wiped her puffy eyes and stood up to greet them.

"Mom, tell them what he did!" I screamed as I joined them in the family room.

"Calm down," the officer began. "Tell me what happened."

Before I could speak, my mother's voice filled the room.

"It's nothing. He's just overreacting," she said, glancing at me. "We were arguing, but Dave never laid a hand on me."

"Yes he did!" I shouted, tears streaming down my cheeks.

"Chip, let your mother talk," my father said calmly. "You know teenagers and all the drama. Look, I'm David St. Clair, ex–Green Beret captain. Say, you look like you were in the military. Let me guess—Marines?"

One of the officers ran his hand across the stubble on his almost completely shaved head.

"Yeah, I did three years in the Corps."

"You look like it. Look like a big, strong guy."

The other officer who happened to be quite a bit older than his partner smiled broadly at my father.

"He may be big, but I could still take him."

"Ha! Hey, how 'bout some coffee?" my father gestured.

"Are you kidding?" I hollered. "Mom, tell them that he does this all the time! Tell them!"

"Look, son," the older officer began, "if you feel like you're in danger, you can leave."

"Yeah, Chip," my father added with sparkling eyes, "you can run to Lisa's."

My father's expression was a mix of victory and defiance. His eyes warned me to shut up and retreat to my room, which I did. I realized that it had been a mistake to call the police. It only made matters worse. The police had come knocking at our door several times throughout my life, probably as a result of neighbors calling to complain about the sounds of violence from our apartment, but the officers always left without pressing charges, under the impression that it was nothing but an innocent family quarrel.

*Perhaps I was overreacting,* I thought.

The night before I left for college, Lisa and I sat in a moonlit parking lot. I had been accepted to Michigan State
University, but had no idea what I wanted to major in. A part
of me wanted to wait for Lisa, who was a year younger. My
father reminded me it was in my best interest to pursue my
education as soon as possible, assuring me that I'd decide what
I wanted to do when I got there. All I knew was that it was
going to be difficult to leave her behind. After a long silence,
Lisa finally spoke up.

"I really care about you, Chip. I love you. But you're going to
be so far away. There are so many people up at college. I hope
you don't forget about me."

I glanced over as she lowered her head. The silver moonlight
played upon the tears on her cheeks.

"It won't be that bad. It's only one year, and then you'll be up
there with me."

"I know. But what if you waited for me?"

"What? Now you don't want me to get an education?" I
asked.

"I do, it's just . . . long-distance relationships usually don't
work. I don't want to lose you."

"Why do you wanna argue on my last night here?"

Raising her hands to her face, Lisa started to sob. I sat
emotionless and unfeeling, waiting for her to finish. *Was this
manipulation, too?*

"Chip," she said, lifting her head, "I want you to be happy, and if we're meant to be together, then nothing can tear us apart. You mean so much to me, and I'm just going to have faith. I know you love me."

"I do," I said softly, gazing at the large moon above.

Autumn leaves rolled past my window while I sat in my dorm room waiting. My mother had called hours earlier, pleading with me to return home. She said my father had gone berserk and she was afraid to be alone. As the end of my first semester of college approached, the phone calls became more frequent. It was either my mother calling because she was being beaten or my father calling, complaining about heart trouble. During my first weekend at college, he had suffered a heart attack. From that time on, he called regularly to alert me of any abnormal discomfort—*Yeah, I've been short of breath all morning and my left arm is getting numb*—followed by a detailed description of every single symptom he suffered since the heartbreak of my abandoning him. *You're up there living your own life. Don't worry about me, I'll just pop some nitro tablets.* Returning home on weekends was like a tug-of-war between my parents and Lisa.

*She's trying to distract you so you flunk out.*

*I was looking forward to spending time with you, Chip. I know your dad needs you, but I miss you, too.*

Between the upsetting phone calls from my parents and missing classes because I was constantly going home, I was flunking out. Since I'd been a fairly good student in high school and had scored high on my college entrance exams, it was frustrating to do so poorly. As I waited for my mother to pick me up that Wednesday morning, I was missing even more classes.

*She should be outside soon,* I thought as I checked my watch.

As I stood up to leave, the phone rang. I set my duffel bag on the tile floor of the small room and pressed the receiver to my ear.

"Hello?"

"Yes, may I speak with Chip St. Clair?" a woman asked.

"This is Chip."

"Hello, Chip. I'm calling from the financial aid department of Michigan State University. Your tuition is over thirty days late."

"Oh," I began uncomfortably. "My mother told me it was paid. I'll check with her about it. Could I call you back?"

"Yes, but please do so within ten days."

"Alright. Good-bye."

That was the third phone call I had received regarding my tuition, which was odd because my mother had borrowed the money for that very purpose from my Aunt Chris. I decided to ask her about it again as I made my way out of the dorm.

"Look who I brought," my mother said, motioning to the passenger seat.

Approaching the car, I leaned down to see what she was

talking about. A smile crossed my face when I realized who it was.

"Lisa! What are you doing here?"

"Your mom called and wondered if I wanted to come along."

"Quit yapping and get in, Chip," barked my mother.

Swinging open the back door, I climbed in.

"I'm really happy you came," I told Lisa, resting my hand on her shoulder. "By the way, Mom, I got another call from the university about my tuition."

"I know," she sighed. "I'm trying to get the money from Aunt Chris. If she doesn't have it, then I'll have to borrow against our car."

"But what about the student loans?"

"They barely covered your books."

"What about the grants?"

She shook her head. "I never mailed in the applications, Chip. The amount was so small, it was hardly worth the effort."

My mother smiled at me in the rearview mirror as we drove through the campus. "Don't be a worrywart," she said. "I'll take care of it by the end of the week."

"But—"

"That's enough," my mother interjected. "Lisa and I were having a nice talk before you came along. Isn't that right, Lisa?"

"Yeah," she agreed.

I settled back into the seat and tried to relax. My mother didn't seem very concerned, so why should I?

My mother and Lisa talked and laughed as we made the long

journey home. I focused less on the content of their conversation and more on their interaction. They looked like they'd been friends for years. I smiled to myself with relief. I never would have believed it, since a few months earlier my mother had shown such contempt for Lisa that I thought the relationship was irreparable.

❦

During the summer, Lisa's father, an avid golfer, had taken us to play a few rounds on the local course. From then on, whenever Lisa and I could grab a few extra hours, we hit the greens. I was mesmerized by the challenge of getting a minuscule white ball into a hole hundreds of yards away in as few strokes as possible.

So it was no great surprise when I asked Lisa if we could go golfing on my birthday. Unfortunately, Lisa had had foot surgery the week before, making walking—much less golfing—an enormous struggle.

*I'll bet she won't even go golfing with you,* my father predicted as I prepared to see her on the morning of my birthday.

I explained to him about her foot and how much pain she was in.

*It doesn't matter,* he spewed toxically, shaking his head. *If she really loves you, she would take you golfing. She's just selfish. Wait and see . . .*

Minutes later I arrived at Lisa's house and was let in by her father. I found her closed in the bathroom, apparently struggling with even the simplest of tasks.

*Hi, Lisa, I'm out here.*

*Hi! Just a minute, I can't get around very well with this cast.*

Remembering my father's prediction, I gave her the opportunity to prove him wrong.

*So, are we golfing today?*

*I really want to,* she explained, *but I don't think I can with my foot. It's throbbing and—*

*I knew it!* I sneered.

*But I do want to,* she argued, *just not today. Couldn't we do something else for your birthday, and maybe golf next week?*

*No!* I exclaimed. *You're being selfish!*

*You're the one who's being selfish! I. . . .*

Before she could finish, I ran out of the house. Hopping into my parents' station wagon, I skidded across the gravel driveway, backing away from the house, away from Lisa.

As I drove aimlessly around the city, I tried sorting through things in my mind. My father always seemed to be able to predict Lisa's reactions. Maybe he was right and I was blind to her underlying intentions. I finally decided to spend the night at my friend's house. The next morning, I awoke on the floor in Nick's bedroom. I searched the darkened room for a clock and saw that it was a little after ten. Nick was a late sleeper, so I quietly got dressed and slipped from the bedroom to kill time until he got up.

Tiptoeing through the house, I reached the living room, and, to my surprise, spotted Lisa's car parked out front. There she sat in the driver's seat with her head resting on the steering wheel. As annoyed as I was that she was outside, a part of me was glad to see her. Whenever I was with her, something inside me felt whole.

Scribbling a quick note to Nick, I unlocked the deadbolt to the front door and went outside. As I approached the car, I saw Lisa's head rise slowly. She was wearing a slight smile on her tired face.

We talked for quite some time, and I realized how unfair it was—birthday or not—to expect her to golf in her current condition. Once again, I had misjudged Lisa and underestimated her intentions and devotion to me.

Knowing my parents would probably be wondering why I wasn't at Nick's house, I asked her to drive me home. Just before making the left turn into my subdivision, I saw my parents' blue station wagon roll slowly by in the opposite lane. My father brought the car nearly to a stop as he wildly rolled down his window.

*You!* he pointed. *Home!*

My heart was in my throat as Lisa made the final turn onto the street leading to my house.

*Are you gonna be okay?* she asked worriedly.

*I don't know.*

I watched anxiously as my father sped up the driveway and slammed the car into park, causing it to rock back and forth. I crossed the lawn on the way to the front porch, when suddenly my mother burst from the car. With arms flailing wickedly, she let out a bloodcurdling scream.

*You bitch!* She jabbed a long, bony finger at Lisa. *You fuck with my baby and I'll kill you! I'll kill you, bitch!*

I turned back to see the horror on Lisa's face. What my mother had said struck Lisa like a physical blow. I could see the pain in her eyes. At my urging, she slowly and reluctantly pulled away.

*Get in the fucking house,* my father growled. *I thought you were through with her. You're such a fucking wimp!*

So from the backseat where I now sat, the merry conversation between Lisa and my mother seemed altogether unnatural. A good-natured, forgiving person, Lisa had apparently swallowed her pride as she erupted into heartfelt laughter, her eyes glowing with happiness. My mother, however, I knew to hold a grudge.

After a long inhale, my mother glanced at me from behind her cigarette through the rearview mirror.

"What are you lookin' at, dickhead?"

I rolled my eyes and fixed my stare at the world speeding by in a blur.

*Perhaps time does heal all wounds,* I thought as laughter resounded in the car.

"You guys be good while I'm gone. I'll only be an hour or so. If I don't get the groceries to start dinner, we'll all be fucked," my mother said as she closed the door to the apartment.

I took my shoes off after the lengthy ride and motioned for Lisa to do the same.

"I'm glad you came," I said, nestling down into the sofa.

"Me, too," she responded as her eyebrows wrinkled. "Where did you guys get this furniture?"

"It came with the place because it's a model. When we moved to this apartment last month, my folks got rid of everything in that other place."

"Chip, how many times have you moved?"

"This year?"

"No, in your life?"

"I think that this makes twenty-four. Or maybe it's twenty-three. . . . I can't remember."

"My gosh! I've lived in the same house for years."

"The longest I've ever lived anywhere was two years."

"That's awful," she said, sitting down beside me. "I can't imagine the feeling of not knowing where I'll wake up next."

"I guess so," I said uncomfortably. "Can we talk about something else?"

"Sure," she said, stroking my hair slowly. "Your mom told me the most unbelievable thing. Did she ever tell you about her dad, or her childhood?"

"No, why?"

"Wow, I really hurt for her. I was happy she was opening up to me," Lisa began, "but, well, I guess her father . . . molested and raped her and her sisters."

"What!" I cried.

"Isn't that horrible? I was crying while she was telling me. She said when she was six years old, someone had turned her father in. When the police were on their way to arrest him, not wanting to go to jail, he went out into the garage, sat in the car, . . . and shot himself in the head."

*Why didn't she ever tell me?*

"Oh, my God! What about her mother? What did she do?"

"Nothing. Whenever your mom would go to her, she would get slapped and sent to her room."

Lisa took in a deep breath and then continued in a very solemn tone. "Her mother made her clean up the blood and brains in the car. She made a *six-year-old* clean up after her own father had committed suicide!"

I rested my hand on Lisa's and patted it as she sobbed into my shoulder. I had no idea my mother had suffered such brutality. I wondered if my father knew her secret. Through all the sadness and torment, there was a small place in my mind that was happy. Happy that my mother had someone to confide in, and happy that that someone was Lisa.

# CHAPTER 10

# Rite of Passage

I TOOK SOME TIME off in my second year of college because my parents needed me to help out with the family finances. While I dreaded the thought of living with them again, I felt a twinge of relief because the struggle of studying through the disturbing phone calls and distractions was taking its toll. I felt as if I were slowly, gruesomely being strangled at the end of a noose. Although I switched my major from astrophysics to political science/prelaw, concentration at the level needed to grasp the subjects proved impossible.

By this time, Lisa had graduated from high school and was now attending the same university, but I still felt little relief. The barrage of phone calls and guilt-trips from my parents never seemed to let up.

A year or so later, my parents began managing another townhouse complex in Auburn Hills, Michigan. They got me a job in the maintenance department, and I worked days for them doing menial jobs, while a few nights a week Lisa and I took classes at a local community college. She had left the university when I did, shelving her own education in an effort to support me. She eventually began working for an insurance company near her home, and when we were not working or going to classes, I managed to steal a few moments to drive over and visit her.

I marveled at the leisurely way in which her parents tackled problems. There was no beating, berating, or screaming; everyone seemed well-mannered and respectful. And although I didn't understand him completely, I recognized that Lisa's father was a kind man. Being with them felt entirely unnatural. To my parents' dismay, I found myself spending a few nights a week at Lisa's home.

*Do what you want. You're the big adult now,* my father would say.

Thus began the purging of poison, the process of distancing myself from my parents. I was slowly transforming my relationship with them from one of dependence to one of independence, which was extremely difficult. I had grown up with abuse all my life, and naturally I expected and accepted what was familiar.

Lisa and her family had opened my eyes to a wholly different perspective on life and relationships, one in stark contrast to what I had always known. I found it difficult to travel backward, to visit my parents with the usual measure of tolerance. But something still gnawed at me, anchoring my mind to the constant dilemma: Which way was the right one, the true path?

More and more of my belongings migrated to Lisa's home. The next step was to secure an independent form of transportation. I no longer felt comfortable using my parents' car, and it wasn't fair to always borrow from Lisa's family. So early one morning, Lisa and I strolled through a car dealership parking lot on a quest for a vehicle that fit our budget.

"How about that one?" asked Lisa, pointing over rows and rows of new and used cars.

Following the line of her index finger, I immediately saw it: a brand-new, bright red Mustang.

"That's a Mustang," I nodded in awe.

"Oh, I didn't realize that," she said. "So why don't we get it?"

"Because," I shook my head, "it's probably a lot more than we could afford."

"Well, how do you know if we don't ask?"

My dependence, my attachment, and the sway my parents held over me were finally beginning to wane.

# CHAPTER
## 11

# Revelations

THE MUSTANG REVVED WHILE I pumped the gas pedal to warm the engine. Cold air spewed forth from the vents until finally the heating mechanism became warm enough to make the air feel comfortable. Though I had only a few hundred yards to drive to my parents' apartment, I still felt like letting the car warm up completely. I was stalling. I wasn't looking forward to an evening spent ignoring the pile of beer cans polished off by my mother, or the spring-loaded demeanor of my father—especially not on Lisa's birthday. Despite my reservations, I put the car in reverse and backed up from the carport, following the road to their townhouse. Nearly every window in the townhouse faced the parking lot, but the only one with the blinds pulled up was the kitchen, to the right of the front door.

I stared at the street address: 113. I wondered why my mother was living in a house with that ill-fated number. Had she given up on superstition, on bad luck?

Lisa and I were walking toward the house, hand-in-hand, when my mother threw open the door.

"Happy birthday, honey," she said, kissing Lisa as we passed through the doorway.

We put our shoes neatly on the doormat and then Lisa kneeled to greet Beau, my parents' seven-year-old poodle.

"Hi, kids," my father said without looking up from his crossword puzzle. "Happy birthday, Lisa."

"Thanks," she smiled, taking a seat across from him.

I pulled out a chair and sat with Lisa to my right and my father to my left. My mother eventually joined us, taking her place across from me.

"You burned the fucker!" my father shouted, looking at the bubbling tray of lasagna in the center of the table.

"It's not burned," my mother protested through eyes glazed over from hours of drinking. "It's fine. I'll eat this. It's the best part!"

Reaching over, she pinched a blackened mound of cheese from the top and slurped it into her mouth. Lisa broke into laughter, but I could tell by my father's eyes that it was no time to laugh. I nudged her slightly with my foot. She got the hint and looked down.

The tension in the room was unbelievably thick. It was almost like an energy, an electricity you could feel, even taste. I had witnessed this sort of calm before the storm many times before, but this felt *different*. The energy seemed to take control of me, trying to ignite me, guide me.

"Did you hear anything new about President Clinton?" my mother garbled through a mouthful of lasagna.

"Who gives a damn," my father barked. "He's the president of the United States. He can do whatever he damn well pleases with interns or anyone else for that matter."

"But doesn't that show something about his overall integrity?"

"No! The man can do what he wants in his private life. It's none of our business!"

"I think it is our business," I said, feeling suddenly electrified.

"Oh, you do, huh?" my father challenged, putting down his fork.

"It's not our business, Chip," my mother mumbled.

I stared at her for a moment and watched the conglomeration of colors being mashed in her open mouth, then turned back to my father.

"If he can't keep a promise or his integrity intact for his own wife, how can he do it for his country?" I pointed out, ignoring Lisa's barrage of kicking protests under the table.

"So *you* are going to tell *me*, who fought and bled for this country, how the president can act? You're way fucking out of line, Jack!"

"I'm just trying to say—"

"I know what you're trying to say, you little naïve prick. You don't know how the goddamn world works, so shut your fucking mouth!"

Placing her hand upon my knee, Lisa whispered, "Chip."

I could feel the adrenaline pumping; my blood pressure was skyrocketing. I couldn't believe his nerve to talk to me that way in front of Lisa.

"You're just a pussy! You don't know shit," he sneered, jabbing a fat finger in my face. "What's wrong with a man havin' a woman on the side? What's so wrong? I spilled my fucking guts for this country so you could be a mouthy little asshole, and you're going to tell *me* about life. You—"

A vein in my neck was pounding. My face flushed with years of contempt boiling just below the surface. I was a dam about to burst. Looking at his face and that familiar condescending, mocking, hateful expression, I gritted my teeth and backhanded an empty pop can off the table. Leaping to my feet, I headed for the front door.

"I'm done. Come on, Lisa."

What happened next was like a dream or a nightmare; everything became suddenly surreal.

"Hey!" my father shouted as I passed down the hallway toward the foyer.

I heard a bounding noise coming in my direction and turned to see what was happening. Before my eyes even met his, my father had his hands around my throat and was pressing his thumbs into my windpipe, squeezing off life's breath. His mouth was stretched into a menacing scowl, and his eyes were like those of a rabid beast with only one goal—to kill. His momentum sent us both past the foyer into the living room, where I desperately tried to peel his crushing fingers from my throat. As I managed to loosen his hands, he leaned back and swung a fist at my face. I lowered my head so the brunt of the force was at my hairline. We plowed through the living room, falling over an end table. Even as we hit the ground, he continued to pummel my head with hard, hammering blows. Having been caught completely off-guard, I could not recover my balance or my wits enough to fight back. My only concern was to survive. With a sudden burst of strength, I wrestled him backward onto a loveseat. Clutching at my shirt, he pulled me down with him. Pinning my face to his chest, he continued to rock my head with blows. I felt each impact, but I couldn't feel the pain, not yet. As I struggled to pull away from him, my father landed a well-placed punch to my right shoulder. I had felt several forms of physical abuse in my twenty-two years, but nothing like what I experienced at that moment. I heard a loud crunching sound as my entire right arm went numb. I screamed in agony and instinctively bit his chest, forcing him to free me, and with a yelp he thrust me back. Bracing my dangling arm, I put distance between us by lurching behind the coffee table in the center of the room. He attempted another lunge at me, but my mother jumped in his path.

"Dave, stop! You're gonna kill him!"

With incoherent words, he grabbed her by the throat and swung a fist at her, knocking her onto the loveseat. I was waiting for my opportunity to make a run for it, but he immediately turned his attention back to me. Lisa stepped from the kitchen and cried out when she caught sight of my arm.

"Shut up!" my father roared, charging toward her.

Without thinking, I jumped between them.

"Just let us go! I need to go to the hospital! Please, let us go!" I cried.

"You hurt his arm, Dave. Let them go!" my mother implored.

I quickly leaned over to pick up my shoes.

"Lisa, grab your shoes and let's go," I shouted.

I swung open the door and was met by a bitter, cold wind. Lisa and I ran ahead, not daring to stop until we reached our car. I didn't look back.

"I called the police," she said as I struggled to get my shoes on with one arm, fighting back tears and the excruciating pain in my shoulder.

My brain finally registered the droning sirens in the background.

"Let's meet them in the parking lot," I suggested, holding my arm against my chest.

"If I ever see you again," my father bellowed from the front door, "I'll kill you!"

Placing her arm around my waist, Lisa led me away from the townhouse. The squeal of the sirens was closing in when I heard my mother call out. She was standing on the sidewalk just outside of the front door, holding herself to keep warm.

"It's okay! He's calmed down. Come on back inside."

"I called the police, Leslie!" Lisa yelled back.

"You did what?!" she said as she threw up her hands. "It's over . . . it's all over!"

At that second, police car upon police car sped to our rescue. A fire truck followed not far behind. A few officers escorted me to the fire truck while others quickly bolted into my parents' townhouse.

"Looks like a dislocation. And a bad one," a fireman said, studying my injury.

Soon an ambulance was on the scene with paramedics helping me into the back to lie down.

"We're taking you and your girlfriend to the hospital. We'll take good care of you, don't worry," a man in a white paramedic's uniform said calmly.

During the next twenty minutes, the paramedics stabilized my arm while the police asked me to explain what happened. As I talked, I could hear Lisa in the front of the ambulance telling the police her version. I looked out the window to see flashing lights beating their red and blue pattern in the dark parking lot. Driving away in the ambulance on that cold January night, I knew my life had changed forever.

My head was throbbing as the impact of the blunt trauma I had suffered set in. I lay in a cool, bright hospital room, nursing my dislocated shoulder, when Lisa suddenly pulled the curtain aside.

"How are you doing?" she asked sympathetically, sitting on the edge of the bed.

"I don't know what hurts worse—my head, my shoulder, or my heart. I can't believe this is happening."

"This stops here," she said firmly. "We have to press charges. He's in jail, you know."

"Really?"

"Yeah, I just called the police department. You won't believe what they told me."

"What? What did they say?"

"This female officer explains to me that he was arrested for domestic violence. I tell her that we are afraid of him getting out and doing this again, or possibly worse. She says that if I call the police again, and he's not found to be doing anything wrong, *I'll* go to jail. Can you believe her nerve? *Me!* How could she threaten me like that after what just happened?"

I knew how. My parents probably knew the officer, along with the entire police department. As managers of an apartment complex, they were in constant contact with the police over resident disputes and other matters. They probably knew most of the police on a first-name basis.

"I called your mom, too."

"You did? What did she say?"

"I told her you are lying in a hospital bed after what her husband did. I told her to leave him, not to take the abuse anymore. What does she say? She's getting an attorney. Not to *help* you, but to *sue* you for biting your dad!"

That night, we returned to our apartment, feeling dazed and completely confused.

*Why was my mother defending him?* I thought. *Why did he snap like that?*

Nothing made sense, but at the same time it did. This was nothing new. He just happened to injure me badly enough this time to require hospital care. How had I dealt with it all of those years? How had my mother? The better question was "why?" Whatever the answers, I knew I could never sit next to him again. Not after this. Not after he'd been put in jail. I was certain he despised me as much as I did him.

"I'm going to call Aunt Chris," I said, reaching awkwardly for the phone with my left arm.

I pushed the familiar sequence of numbers that I had dialed whenever violence erupted. Sometimes she could calm him down or at least rattle his conscience to some degree.

"Hello?" My aunt finally answered after quite a few rings.

I was surprised to hear her voice so alert at 1:00 AM, for I had expected to awaken her.

"Aunt Chris? It's Chip. I've really got a problem."

"I know, I just got off the phone with your mother."

"She's going to sue me!"

"She's really worried, Chip. There is something you should know. You can't tell anyone . . . not even Lisa."

"O-okay," I began, confused, waving Lisa over to listen.

"Your father," she paused, "his name isn't David St. Clair."

My breath was still.

"His real name is Michael Dean Grant. He's a fugitive."

My jaw dropped, but I said nothing.

"He killed a child in 1970. He escaped from prison in 1973 . . . with the help of your mother."

The years of abuse, the torture, the beatings, the fear. . . . My mind immediately flooded with a million questions. I asked but one.

"Was he ever in Vietnam?"

She took in a deep breath, then sighed.

"No. He dropped out of high school when he was sixteen. Our mother lied for him and said he was seventeen so he could join the army. After about three or four weeks, he went AWOL."

"Unbelievable," was all I could manage to say.

*He never was in Vietnam . . . the anguish, the rage, the tears . . . the scar on his abdomen, a child murderer.*

I looked at Lisa in disbelief. Her face reflected the shock in my own. All those years I had justified the violence, the unpredictability. I thought he had post-traumatic stress disorder from his wartime service. In my mind I had rationalized his behavior as a response to all the terror and bloodshed he'd witnessed half a world away. *That's what had caused him to lose his sanity,* I would tell myself. Now the truth: He was nothing more than a vicious, brutal, child murderer—not a war hero.

"Chip?" my aunt asked.

Shadows, questions from the past, began materializing in my mind.

*Were there signs that I could have spotted? Clues I missed?*

I was about six years old when his mother died of cancer. I remember that my mother and I attended the funeral in Indiana, but my father didn't come.

*So, you're Mickey's boy?* I remember someone asking.

*Mickey? Who's Mickey?* I thought.

*So, whereabouts are you living now? Where do you go to school?*

Before I could answer, my mother had grabbed me by the arm and whisked me away.

"Chip?"

"Yeah, I'm here. I just don't know what to say. Where did the name St. Clair come from?"

"I don't know. They made it up, I guess. Just like they made up Carole."

"Carole?"

"That's the name they took when he escaped on November 16, 1973."

"November 16, 1973! That was their wedding anniversary!"

"They were never married. Leslie delivered mail to our mother, your grandmother, in Elkhart, Indiana. In a small town, people get to know one another. Your mother eventually asked who was sending letters from prison. When your grandmother explained that Michael had no one to visit him, Leslie offered to go. Apparently, Leslie began visiting him in prison, they coordinated an escape, and on November 16, 1973, she picked him up on the highway during a work detail."

The room began to spin.

"What's *my* name?" I asked quietly.

"I-I don't . . . it's Chip. You'll always be Chip."

*That's why my father could never show a driver's license. . . . That's why I never saw any wedding pictures. They were fugitives, on the run for twenty-six years!*

"Your mother is scared he'll be found out. You can't tell anyone."

*What would you do if you found out I had been to prison?* His haunting words were seared into my soul.

Then, another thought, another shade crept from the darkness.

*What would you do if you found out you had been kidnapped?*

I tried to ask the question calmly.

"How do you know . . . that I'm their child?"

My aunt paused, then sighed, and then paused again.

"I was there in the delivery room," she said plainly.

"But how do you know that baby was me?"

"I-I just do."

I heard the phone click, which told me another call was coming through on her line.

"That's probably your mom. Can I talk to you later?"

"Yeah."

"Are you okay?"

"I guess so."

The phone clicked.

"Okay?" I said after hanging up. "How the hell can I be

okay?! I just found out my father is an escaped child murderer and my mother was the getaway driver! How do you think I feel?! I don't even know who I am or what my real name is!"

Fate had dealt me a wicked hand, and I had the longest night of my life deciding which card to play next.

We sat awake into the early morning hours, digesting what we had just heard. I tried not to believe it and told myself it hadn't happened. The threads of my reality were unraveling; everything I had thought was true was exposed as lie after lie. I thought back to all the war stories he had cried about. His short-lived career as a kicker for the Cincinnati Bengals—a lie. A stock car racer—a lie. The medals of honor, battle scars, rank, and serial number—all lies.

Maybe that was why I never went to doctors. I remember once, when I was fourteen, I was embroiled in a pick-up football game with some kids in the apartment complex my parents managed. My friend Nick had thrown a lofty pass, and when I leapt up to grab it, I came down hard on a fallen tree branch. Several kids heard the loud snap, and as I held my right ankle, writhing in agony, all of them realized it wasn't the branch that had broken.

Nick and a few others helped me home, and as I hobbled in, my father scoffed.

*Oh, you pussy! What did you do?*

*My leg, or my ankle. I think it's broken.* I winced as I dragged myself to a chair in the kitchen.

*Oh, bullshit. It's probably just a sprain. Let me have a look.*

*Ahhh!* I moaned as he moved my foot up and down.

*Let me look at it, damn it! I treated shit worse than this in Vietnam. You're such a fucking baby.*

I bit my lip while he continued to inspect it.

*Yep. It's a sprain. Just wrap it up. Keep ice on it, and you'll be fine.*

For three days I hobbled to and from the bus stop, and all around school, with a foot that looked as if someone had sewn a softball inside it. Eventually, a teacher spotted it and sent me to the school nurse. A doctor visit, ordered by the nurse, revealed that my ankle had been badly fractured.

His medical training in the army, a POW in Vietnam—lies. And of all things, a child murderer! *Who did he kill, and why?*

Remembering Lake Michigan and my terror on the balcony of International Towers in California, I wondered if he had been trying to kill me, too. My mother, my grandmother, my aunt—they all knew his secret. I felt so alone, so orphaned.

Lisa called her brother, Ryan, to keep us company. Her parents were out of town because her mother was undergoing surgery. Time ticked slowly by, leaving each of us to our thoughts. My mind floated back to my childhood. Every memory, every experience, seemed different, for I was seeing them with different eyes—the eyes of truth. Yet even with all I had learned, there remained so many unanswered questions. I decided to visit my mother in the morning to confront her about other secrets she might still hold.

"What if they let him go?" Lisa said softly, breaking the silence.

"They'll check his fingerprints," Ryan pointed out. "The police probably already know who he is."

"But what if they don't? I'm afraid he'll get out," Lisa said, looking over to me.

"And finish the job," I said as I began to rub my throbbing shoulder.

"He killed someone's child! My God, Chip, he could have killed you at any time!"

"I know."

"He needs to be behind bars. Some of the things you told me about your childhood make sense now. He was dangerous. He *is* dangerous."

"I think he tried to kill me sometimes. Other times he just liked to torture me."

"You were his puppet, his punching bag."

Lisa was right. He had me eating out of his hand. I wasn't trying to please him out of love, as I had always believed, but out of one of the most powerful forces in nature: fear. I tried to impress him, to make him happy, to do whatever he asked because I was *afraid* of him.

"You have to call," Lisa said resolutely.

I pictured him sitting in jail surrounded by concrete walls and cold bars. A part of me cried out to help him. A twinge of guilt gnawed at my brain.

*How can you let me rot here?* I could almost hear him say.

"Lisa," I began, "why do I feel this way? Why do I feel guilty?"

"Because he warped your mind. He abused you your entire life. Look at your arm, Chip!" Lisa cried.

"He probably is blaming *me*, not himself. You're right, he's got to be stopped. He has to take responsibility for his actions," I said, reaching for the phone.

"Auburn Hills Police," stated the voice on the other end.

"This is Chip St. Clair," I said. "I need to know the status of someone you have in custody."

The officer requested the case number and then transferred me to a detective.

"Detective Shaw here."

"Uh, this is Chip St. Clair. I wanted to know the status on David St. Clair."

"He's done being processed," the detective said simply. "He doesn't have any prior record, so he'll be released in a couple of hours."

My hands began to tremble uncontrollably. What I was about to do would not only seal my father's fate, but my own. The Shakespearean dramas I had devoured throughout my life were springing to life. Blood against blood. Good versus evil. Fate had indeed dealt me a wicked hand.

"Did you take his fingerprints?"

"Sure we did."

"Did you check them through your computer?"

"No. We don't run prints unless there's a reason."

"Well, you have a reason," I sighed.

"W-what do you mean?" the detective asked anxiously.

"His name isn't David St. Clair," I said with great effort. "It's . . . Michael Grant. He's a fugitive who escaped from Indiana State Prison back in 1973."

"We have Michael Grant in custody?" he shouted. "He's one of Michigan's ten most wanted!"

I continued relaying all the information that Aunt Chris had told me. Detective Shaw stated that Michael Grant would most likely be extradited back down to Indiana, where he would serve the remainder of his sentence. Before I hung up, I asked him not to mention that I had informed the police.

"Just say it was anonymous."

*That's what I am, anonymous. Even to myself.*

I found my mother a frazzled mess a few hours later. She apparently had slept no more than I had, but for different reasons. She wasn't wrestling with how to do the *right* thing. As she had done her whole life, my mother was trying to figure out how to keep doing the *wrong* thing. Her skin was pale and wrinkled. She looked as if she had aged ten years overnight. As Lisa and I entered her apartment, she was hanging up the phone.

"Did the police tell you?" she asked simply, a cigarette wagging loosely in her mouth.

"Yeah," I lied.

"I just got off the phone with my boss. They don't know anything yet, and I want to keep it that way. I need to keep our job here, at least until he gets out."

"I don't think he's getting out," I said.

"Oh, I'll get him out. I already called an attorney. I just told our boss he had a heart attack and is getting some R&R in Indiana."

"We need to talk," I said, walking past her into the kitchen.

We took seats around the table as we had the night before, the night I unknowingly plunged into my destiny.

"I have some questions I ne—"

"I don't have time. I have to get to—"

"Mom!" I shouted. "You deprived me of the truth my entire life. The least you could do is answer a couple questions before you tend to the man who did *this*!"

Removing the coat that blanketed my shoulders, I exposed the sling that held my arm.

"How long do you have to wear it?" she asked, trying to sound concerned.

"It doesn't matter," I said, leaning across the table to stare at her intently. "Whose child did he kill?"

"I don't know," she began, breaking the stare. "We never talked about it."

"You *never* talked about it?"

"We began writing when he was in prison. We used a code because the bastards read every letter. After he was denied parole, we coordinated an escape plan. He had been granted trustee status and could work outside the prison on the roads."

My mother's face brightened into a wide smile. "One morning while he was working on a highway, I came by in a white Wildcat and picked him up. That's when we began our twenty-six-year adventure!"

"*Adventure?* He was a child murderer! Look what he did to me all those years! Look what he did to you!"

"Leslie," Lisa began patiently, "this is your chance. Let him go. We'll help you. He's dangerous!"

My mother stared out the large window next to the table. Her thoughts were very far away. I almost pitied her—the dark bags beneath her eyes, her cheek swollen from the beating the night before. Yet I couldn't help but resent her. What person in her right mind breaks a man out of prison, commits God knows what other crimes, knows the pain of abuse, and yet forces her child to endure the same torture?

"I vowed never to leave him," she said coldly, her gaze steady. "And I will be with him till the end."

"He doesn't give a shit about you," I retorted. "He nearly beat you to death dozens of times."

"He never laid a hand on me."

Lisa opened her mouth to speak, but I held up my hand for her to stop. My mother was as ill as my father.

"I can't make you respect yourself, but at least give *me* an ounce of respect."

My mother rose to her feet and glided to the refrigerator to pull out a can of beer and then took her seat once again.

"Go ahead, shoot," she said, cracking open the can.

"Was I kidnapped?"

"What do you think—I took you from a Kmart?"

I looked over at Lisa as she raised her eyebrows.

"Are you my mother?"

"You call me 'Mom,' don't you?"

"Where did the name Carole come from?"

"That was the name of the nurse who delivered you. I couldn't use my name or your father's, so I just read it off of her name-tag," she said smugly, raising the can of beer to her lips.

"Aunt Chris said that she was in the delivery room when I was born."

"Bullshit. No one else was there."

My mind was reeling. I had thought of a million questions, yet my mother wasn't cooperating, and her evasiveness had thrown me off-track.

"Look," I pleaded, "I just want to know the truth."

"Ha," she chuckled, taking another sip. "You don't know the half of it. I'll tell you guys the whole story someday. Right now, I got shit to do."

Lisa and I could do little else but leave. While I wanted to know more, I was still grappling with an overwhelming amount of information about twenty-two years of lies in the span of only twenty-four hours.

I decided to give my mother some time to herself to think things through. In all honesty, I needed my space as well. I also thought being without Michael Grant for a few days might allow reality to settle in. She needed to realize the danger she was in; she had been sucked in for so long that she couldn't think clearly. He had an uncanny ability to make those around him aim to please, and then feel guilty if their attempts failed. I knew my mother wouldn't open up to me while she remained loyal to Michael Grant, but I hoped in his absence she would have a change of heart. She never did.

"I'm busy right now," my mother slurred, her tongue numb from inebriation.

"I just want some answers," I pleaded.

"Shhh. The phone is tapped."

"No, it's not. Look, can I just come over and talk?"

"You can't now," she said. "I got things to burn."

"What do you mean? What things?"

"Oh, nothing. By the way, I got a letter from your dad today. He's back in Indiana State Prison, ya know?"

"I know, but—"

"Hey, you know what?" she paused for a loud belch. "'Scuse me. Ya know the jeans he wore all the time?"

"The ones that were always starched and ironed?"

"That's them. Do you know why they were his favorite?" she asked slyly.

"No, why?"

"'Cuz those are the ones he escaped prison in! All those years

I ironed them and mended them in front of you, and you never knew! Ha!"

"That's not funny! You don't even realize the impact of what you guys have done to me. I—"

"Anyway, you'd be very proud of your dad if you heard some of his prison stories. He was a real bad-ass. Once, he—"

"How could he have been a bad-ass?" I snapped. "There were no women or children to beat!"

"I gotta go," my mother said, slamming down the phone.

My frustration was unimaginable. She held the answers to all my questions, yet adamantly denied me any information.

I turned to my Aunt Chris for answers, but gained nothing useful from her, either. Her memory of the murder was very vague, and the details she *did* remember contradicted what my mother had said. My mother claimed to be alone in the delivery room when she gave birth to me, yet Aunt Chris said she was there. My mother claimed the surname Carole was inspired by the nurse in the delivery room, while Aunt Chris said she was told it was taken from a close friend of the family. I didn't know whom to believe. The last hope I had was to call my half-brother, Rick, my father's son from a previous marriage. My father had kept this family secret as well, so I figured he had to have some valuable information. Unfortunately, he was too young when the murder occurred to remember anything. Rick had virtually no contact with us except through Aunt Chris, leaving me once again stymied at the entrance to this labyrinth of lies.

When I had him on the phone, however, I couldn't resist the one lingering question.

"How do you know Leslie is my mother?"

"She's the one who raised you, Chip. She's your mother."

That answer just didn't sit right. It wasn't definitive. All these family members knew and perpetrated these lies. They enabled Michael Grant to remain a fugitive by hiding him and covering up for him. They maintained the lies by backing up his stories of service in Vietnam and by calling him "Dave," leaving *me* with the burden of doing the morally correct thing.

"All I ask is for them to give me some peace of mind by answering a few questions, and for whatever reason, they won't," I said, anguish underlying my words.

"We'll find the answers, Chip," Lisa said. "We'll find out what happened, with or without their help."

She was right about one thing: If I needed answers, I was going to have to find them myself.

A phone call shattered the air late one evening, shaking us out of our slumber.

"Chip?" my mother asked in a shaky voice.

I hadn't heard from her for days, and her voice told me something was wrong.

"What's the matter?"

"Beau's dead," she moaned.

"What!"

Lisa couldn't hear what my mother had told me, so I mouthed the words for her. Her face immediately became grief-stricken as she reached for something to steady herself.

My mother was telling me that a dog that was perfectly healthy weeks earlier was dead.

"What happened?" I yelled incredulously.

"He just . . . died."

I abruptly hung up the phone and joined Lisa, who was already putting on her shoes and jacket at the door.

We arrived at my mother's apartment to find her standing in the doorway, holding Beau's tiny, limp body. As I ran from the car, I noticed blood covering my mother's shirt and matted within the fur on Beau's head and chest.

"He's okay," she said, calmly stroking him.

"Give him to me," I growled, taking Beau's lifeless body from her arms.

"Are you sure he's dead?" Lisa sobbed.

"He died around seven," my mother informed us.

"It's 10:30! He's been dead three and a half hours?" I demanded. "Oh, Beau," I cried, imagining the poor animal's last moments.

"You killed him," I sneered, narrowing my eyes at her.

"No, I didn't! Rocky jumped off of the couch onto him and—"

"Rocky only weighs a little more than Beau. He couldn't have killed him. Not with that much blood. I'm taking him to the vet," I said, walking back to the car.

I ran my hand across Beau's soft fur as I drove, trying to block out the images of what might have happened. Lisa was crying uncontrollably, not only because he was dead, but also at the brutal condition the dog appeared to be in. My mother insisted on coming along and sat quietly in the back.

The veterinary hospital was closed, but a receptionist hunched behind the counter to take emergency phone calls. Lisa pounded on the glass door to get her attention.

"We're closed," the woman called through the glass, obviously annoyed that we were distracting her from her magazine.

I stepped in front of Lisa and held out Beau for the woman to see. With mouth gaping, she quickly unlocked the door.

"He's dead," I informed her. "But I didn't know what to do. I want to find out what happened."

The portly woman shuffled behind her station once more and produced a card to fill out.

"Looks like he got hit by a car," the woman said sadly.

I looked over at my mother who was busily filling out the registration card.

"It wasn't a car. He died in *her* house."

"Oh," said the woman, looking down uncomfortably.

"When will the doctor be in?" asked Lisa.

"Around eight or nine tomorrow. Feel free to call back then," the receptionist finished, taking Beau gently from my arms.

"Hold on!" my mother gasped frantically while reaching into her purse.

A small pair of scissors gleamed in the fluorescent light as she cut a lock of fur from Beau's leg.

"There," she said, then tucked the fur deep into her purse.

The maelstrom continued to swirl around me, and while I didn't know for sure what happened that night, I intended to find out as soon as the sun rose.

"What do you mean you can't talk to me about Beau?" I asked in disbelief.

"Your name doesn't appear on the registration card," stated the new receptionist the following morning. "A woman by the name of Leslie Weaver filled it out. She called this morning and told us not to allow anyone access to the animal's records."

"But I believe she may have killed him! I wanted an autopsy perform—"

"Ms. Weaver specifically told us not to perform an autopsy. She told us to hold the animal until such time as she could bury him."

"Thank you," I mumbled, hanging up the phone.

Something was very wrong. I decided to confront my mother directly by calling her at work.

"Westbury Village Townhomes," she said cheerfully.

"Why did you call the vet this morning? What in God's name did you do to Beau?"

"Uh, I can't talk now. I have people sitting in front of me. Let me call you a little later."

"I don't give a damn! You answer my questions now! What happened last night?!"

"I'll call you back. I promise. Just give me a little time," she said before hanging up.

Her voice sounded strained, as if she had been crying.

With patience worn thin, I waited the remainder of the morning for her call. When the phone finally rang, I practically broke my leg running to answer it.

"Hello?" I gasped.

"Chip St. Clair?" inquired a male voice.

"Yes?"

"This is Detective Tucker. I don't know how to tell you this. I know you've been through a lot lately . . ."

"What is it?" I asked, certain that nothing more could shock me.

"We arrested Leslie Weaver today."

"For helping Michael Grant escape?"

"No. Indiana said that they have who they want. We arrested her for embezzlement."

"Embezzlement," I stated, throwing up my hand.

Lisa stood by, eyes widened in amazement.

"Yes, she had apparently been letting residents move into the complex and covered the books so that her company continued to believe that the apartments were vacant. She accepted the residents' checks and cashed them herself."

"They were like Bonnie and Clyde," I stated flatly.

"Maybe so. At any rate, Leslie wants you to come down to

the police station to get the keys to her apartment. She was hoping you could take care of her stuff until she posts bail. She also mentioned there is a dog that needs to be cared for."

"There used to be two dogs, but she killed one last night."

"Oh . . . I wouldn't know anything about that," the detective sighed. "I have to worry about one thing at a time."

"Alright. I'll be right there to get the keys."

"Okay. Just ask for me when you get here."

His voice trailed off to a more whispered tone.

"Hey, Chip, did you ever consider the possibility that you might have been kidnapped?"

Another wretched shadow from the past floated into the room.

*What would you do if you found out you had been kidnapped?* My father had asked so simply.

"Yeah. It's crossed my mind."

# CHAPTER
## 12

# The Moment of Truth

T HE SUN POURED THROUGH a set of semi-opened mini-blinds, barely illuminating my parents' darkened apartment. Rocky, who normally rushed to greet Lisa and me at the door, lay mournfully on the recliner at the opposite end of the living room. As I crossed the dingy carpeting to greet my sad, old friend, I stumbled over snack food wrappers and discarded beer cans. I had never seen my parents' home in such disarray. Michael Grant would *never* have tolerated such chaos—not because he was a neat and orderly person, but because he had a desperate need to control everything around him.

Rocky raised his head and wiggled his tail as I ran my hand over his thick, black fur.

"He's filthy," I said, feeling the dog's greasy, mangled coat.

"So is this place," Lisa said, wrinkling her nose.

Her expression changed as she turned on a light switch.

"Chip! Look at all the blood!"

The limited sunlight concealed evidence of the massacre that had taken place. Dried blood was caked on the carpeting and the sofa. The edge of the coffee table was painted with several smears, while the end table near the foyer revealed a large blood-stain, dripping down the side onto the floor.

"Poor Rocky had to witness the whole thing," I said solemnly.

We traced our way through rooms I had been in hundreds of times, searching through drawers and closets, finding nothing. Although no one was home—nor ever would be again—my heart raced with anxiety. I was looking for something, but I wasn't sure what.

We eventually made our way to the staircase. As we ascended, my legs became heavy, my steps slow and deliberate.

If anything was to be found it would be in the room at the top of the stairs.

"Their bedroom . . . " I whispered.

Reaching the upper landing, I grasped the door handle before I could lose my nerve. With a quick glance at Lisa, I turned the knob and walked in.

The air was stale and musty. Dark shapes and shadows filled the room, for the heavy curtains drawn at the back blotted out all light save that which spilled in through the doorway. Placed neatly at the foot of my parents' bed was a black trunk. It was not hidden. There was no lock, nor was there need for one. My father had ruled by fear, and fear can be more powerful than any lock. I trembled as I stood staring at the trunk. I felt very small, balancing on the razor's edge of darkness and light. I forced myself to kneel before it. The seconds seemed like hours, as my hand rested on its latch. An unnerving quiet hung in the air—the stillness before a storm. I wished I could walk away, but I knew my moment of truth had arrived—that elusive moment that each of us must face, the one that tests our mettle and defines us.

I undid the brass latch and raised the lid.

Worn, faded photographs, official-looking documents, booklets and folders filled the old trunk. I reached in and pulled out a small, pale-green sheet of paper: a birth certificate issued by Elkhart General Hospital in Indiana. The name read "Chip Anthony St. Clair." The father and mother were listed as David and Leslie St. Clair. The birth date was August 1, 1975.

"Oh my gosh," Lisa said, quickly grabbing it from my hands.

She held it overhead so the light from the doorway shone through it.

"It's been typed over! Your birth certificate has been forged!" she cried.

Wanting to see for myself, I held it to the light just as she had. Every single letter had been typed over, and as I looked closer I could make out a hidden name. The name St. Clair had been typed over another one: Carole.

"Chip, here's a collection letter from a student loan company for $18,000!"

"What? She applied for loans in my name?"

"That's not all she did. Look," Lisa said, holding a perforated piece of paper.

"A *scholarship* check? I got a scholarship? Why didn't she tell me?"

"Because she cashed it, that's why! But there's more."

Lisa produced a handful of letters from different collection agencies, credit card companies, and utility companies. Various accounts had been opened in my name and apparently remained in collection for years.

"Looks like they even had an apartment lease in your name," she added.

I began furiously rummaging through the trunk, knowing full well that the more I dug, the more my life would crumble around me. The next few hours in that darkened bedroom unveiled one soul-shattering shock after another. I uncovered school records I never knew existed from preschools I'd never heard of, claiming that "Chip St. Clair" attended two different schools at the same time, nearly one hundred miles apart. I found pictures of two cribs in what appeared to be the same house, pictures of children with the inscription "Chip, five years old" scribbled on the backs.

"Let me see those," said Lisa, snatching the photos.

"What is it?"

"Chip, both of these pictures read 'Chip, five years old,' but they sure don't look like the same child."

I compared the photographs, confirming Lisa's observation. The children definitely appeared to be different. One child had a sad demeanor with a round face, brown eyes, and dark brown hair. The other boy was a little more confident, light hair combed neatly over a large forehead, and wore a bright smile, exposing a long, pointed chin.

As I stared at the pictures in disbelief, Lisa handed me another stack of papers. I sorted through them, uncovering a small, wrinkled envelope with the name Dave written on the front.

"Lisa, this is a letter from my mother to my father," I said, scanning the pages.

"What does it say?" she asked as she moved in to see over my shoulder.

"Don't blow your top," I read from the letter, "but I'm pregnant!"

"Pregnant? When?"

"The letter is dated 1982! I would have been about seven when this was written," I exclaimed. "Listen to this: I promise I won't show until the last minute . . . I'll only miss a couple days of work . . . I'll still be able to take care of the boys . . ."

"Oh my God! What boys?!" Lisa asked, grabbing the letter.

We continued to rummage through the trunk, and I soon came across papers I recognized as autographs from numerous encounters my parents had allegedly had with celebrities. I paused when I found the glossy photo of Mikhail Gorbachev I had so proudly presented to my class when I was younger.

"They all look like Leslie's handwriting," Lisa observed.

I studied the formation of the letters on the autograph and dropped them to the floor.

"It's one thing to cover up who you really are, but it's another to take it *this* far. To make up an entire reality—from rubbing elbows with celebrities to being a highly decorated war hero. Everything I ever knew was a lie! My memories, my thoughts, my opinions—all based on lies. They did so much more than just cover up *who* they were. They took away all I knew as reality. I may have had a rotten childhood, but it was *mine*. I had *my* memories and my thoughts. Now they've left me with nothing. I don't know my name, my birth certificate has been forged, my memories are lies, and I can't even be sure I wasn't kidnapped!"

I fell into Lisa's arms, sobbing. The black trunk held a wealth of answers, but each answer spawned another question.

The months to follow brought nothing but a series of dead ends. Because of the fraudulent student loans and credit cards, my credit rating suffered severely. I went to the local police with my evidence; they sent me to the state police, who, in turn, passed me off to the FBI, who graciously and regretfully informed me that I needed to take it up with the local police. If the problem wasn't jurisdiction, it was the dollar amount being too high for some agencies or too low for others. No one could help me, and I quickly became aware of why identity theft was such a growing concern. And I was the poster child for identity theft, to say the least.

My financial ruin was merely one of the fraying threads in my life. I began pouring my energy into scouring the evidence in the trunk, which was now a prominent fixture in the center of my living room. A fabric of mystery unraveled with each new piece of information. Falsified immunization records for a Chip Carole, doctored Social Security cards for a Chip Carole, and a stack of curious photographs occupied every moment of our spare time. Calls made to verify the forged documents yielded no new information. We were groping blindly for clues, for answers in the midst of an intricate web of lies.

Then it occurred to me that every lie and every truth has a beginning. If I wanted to peel back layer upon layer of fabrication to discover the core truth, I would have to dive into the heart of where it all started. I would need to investigate the circumstances that landed Michael Grant in prison in the first place.

I traveled along the dusty roads of rural Indiana as I had dozens of times before. This time, however, my eyes were wide open, free from the blindfold of deceit.

Lisa and I were able to spare a few days from the cleaning company we'd recently opened. We had decided to make the long trip to Indiana in hopes of returning with a supply of knowledge to feed our insatiable appetite for the truth.

Our list of stops included the public library, police stations, hospitals, and anywhere else we could acquire factual information pertaining to my life. I even contacted Michael Grant's Uncle Tom, whom he had grown up with. Only a few years older than Michael Grant, Tom remembered much about Michael's personality and young adulthood. Apparently they had spent a great deal of time together as children and teenagers, but lost touch when Tom joined the navy. A small town like Elkhart, however, was likely to yield ample gossip and whispering. What Uncle Tom and his family didn't know first-hand most likely made its way back to their ears indirectly.

Before leaving Michigan, I called to introduce myself. He was surprised to hear from me, as we had never met, but even more surprised to learn that Michael Grant was back behind bars. He and his wife Irene warmly invited us to their home and seemed perfectly willing to provide whatever help they could.

The great expanses of corn and wheat fields ended abruptly when we turned from the interstate onto a side road. Quaint farmhouses bordered by several acres of land dotted both sides. Uncle Tom had agreed to meet us at a local gas station and lead us back to his home.

Aside from the unfortunate circumstances of our visit, the brief stay was very pleasant. Two of the kindest people we had ever met provided us with photographs, slides, reels, and story upon story of the adolescent Michael Grant. Irene went out of her way to accommodate us with all the food and hospitality we desired, while Uncle Tom flipped through albums of black-and-white photographs.

I picked his brain from one subject to the next, but was taken aback when he began to speak of the murder. Uncle Tom not only knew the child who had been murdered, but had also been at Michael Grant's trial. A search through public records and old newspaper clippings confirmed Uncle Tom's recollections, but lacked the all-important, minute details that only a privileged few happened to know.

According to Uncle Tom, Michael Grant wasn't much different from other kids his age. He appeared to have normal social skills and average athletic abilities; nothing about him really stood out as unusual or quirky. Michael did, as Tom recalled, have one strange habit: He constantly, almost obsessively, changed his shirt. Tom remembered following him to school one day and catching Michael in an old barn sifting through a stash of shirts. He had been hoarding them at the barn so as not to draw any attention to himself at home. When confronted, Michael admitted to changing his shirt several times a day, which was exactly what I had observed while growing up.

When talk of war in Vietnam captured the attention of America's youth, Michael Grant decided his time would be better spent in the military than in the classroom. After obtaining his mother's permission, as required, he dropped out of high school and joined the army. Only weeks into basic training, Michael Grant left the base, hopped on a bus, and never returned. The U.S. Army fought to mar his record with a dishonorable discharge, but Michael's mother eventually talked them out of it.

He spent the next several years doing odd jobs and dating a few of the local girls. At nineteen, he met a woman by the name of Marilyn, who soon gave birth to a son, Brian. The relationship dissolved shortly after their second son, Rick, was born. Marilyn decided that she and her children needed to escape Michael Grant's violence before it was too late.

He then married a woman named Charlotte, a union that ended abruptly in divorce. The details surrounding the divorce remain unknown.

In his late twenties, Michael got a job as a used car salesman, which suited his personality just fine. He appeared outgoing and friendly at first glance, endearing himself to his supervisors as well as his customers.

It was no wonder when a young divorcée named Sue Balsley fell for Michael's smooth charm and quick wit. Sue, who had an eighteen-month-old son named Jeffrey, eagerly accepted Michael's marriage proposal and promises of a new and wonderful life. But the shiny promises soon tarnished as Michael Grant's brutality seeped through his broad smiles and friendly winks.

She returned home one day to find her baby boy bruised and beaten to death. Only hours earlier he had been in Michael's care. Police named Michael Grant as the prime suspect in little Jeffrey's death, but hit a roadblock when the coroner reversed his findings from "homicide" to "inconclusive." A judge ordered Michael Grant to check himself into a psychiatric hospital, which he reluctantly did. During his brief stay in the hospital, Sue Balsley filed for divorce.

Within weeks of being released, Michael reentered the dating scene. This time he met a young waitress named Vicki

Ingersoll. Vicki had custody of her three- and five-year-old sons and seemed pleased to once again have a man in their lives. They attended functions and family picnics together, but one incident in particular stuck in Uncle Tom's mind like a thorn.

Michael and the two boys were playing near the lake one July afternoon while Vicki was visiting with Tom's family at a group of picnic tables nearby. Tom became distracted from the conversation when he saw Michael slapping Vicki's younger child, Scott. As Tom rushed to the boy's aid, Michael picked up the small child and heaved him into the lake. Fortunately, the boy was quickly rescued and returned to his mother's arms. Michael claimed he was only playing a game with the child, but Tom knew otherwise. He pulled Michael aside and warned him that if he ever saw him abuse the child again, he would receive the beating of a lifetime.

Sadly, neither Tom nor anyone else would be around to help little Scott and Thomas Ingersoll on the night of August 1, 1970.

Vicki had to work the night shift at the restaurant, so Michael was supposed to relieve the boys' babysitter and keep them occupied until she came home. He found the babysitter, who happened to be Vicki's fifteen-year-old brother, in front of the television with the children. Apparently unconcerned about leaving young Scott and Thomas unattended, Michael offered Vicki's brother a ride home.

Michael returned about twenty minutes later and found the boys right where he had left them. He walked over to the television to shut it off, ordering the boys to strip down and get ready for a bath. Michael escorted them into the bathroom with instructions to draw the water and get in. Soon Michael emerged from a bedroom in the rear of the house wearing only his underwear and discovered the brothers playfully splashing in the tub. When he saw that they were sloshing water onto the floor, he became enraged and plunged their heads underwater. Michael grabbed young Scott by the arm and jerked him into the air, frightening the child to the point of involuntary urination. He slapped the boy's small, frightened face and slammed him down onto the cold tile floor. Thomas, who was still in the bathtub, began screaming in terror, diverting Michael's attention from Scott. He punched Thomas in the stomach and then whirled him around, ramming his head through the thick plaster wall.

Scott picked himself up and bolted out of the room toward the front door with Michael trailing close behind. He scooped Scott up as he neared the door and quickly locked the deadbolt. Turning the wriggling, crying child upside down, Michael Grant firmly grasped his ankles. Loud thumps mixed with moans of agony could be heard by Scott Ingersoll as Michael swung the boy's tiny, nude body back and forth like a baseball bat, bashing his head against the walls in the hallway on his way back to the bathroom.

Thomas lay dazed on the floor when his unconscious brother was errantly tossed beside him. A barrage of kicking and stomping ensued until Michael was certain neither boy would survive. Finally realizing what he had done, Michael fled the grotesque scene, wearing little more than blood and underwear.

His parents were staying at a cottage only a few miles away. As in the past, whenever he was in trouble, he turned to his mother. After learning what had taken place, she accompanied her son to the police station to help sort matters out. Michael waited in the car while his mother entered the station and attempted to explain that her son *thought* he had killed someone. She told them that Michael had hallucinated once before, believing he had killed an infant, which she believed to be untrue. As police officers exited the station to question Michael, he sprang from the car and waded into a nearby river to escape. He was eventually apprehended and charged with second-degree murder.

Thomas Ingersoll remained in critical condition for days, but avoided the fate that befell his three-year-old brother. During the trial, the prosecution presented viciously graphic photographs of the crime scene. The boys' little bodies were covered with bruises in the shapes of footprints as a result of the incessant stomping. Small fragments of a thermostat could be seen embedded in the skull of young Scott from the attack in the hallway.

The distraught Thomas testified that even in the days before the murder, Michael Grant had been abusing his brother and him.

Going against his court-appointed attorney's advice, Grant took the stand in his own defense. The ex–used car salesman sold himself to the small-town jury. To everyone's amazement and disappointment, Michael was only convicted of voluntary manslaughter as an alternative to second-degree murder. He was sentenced to two to twenty-one years in Indiana State Prison.

"I don't know how the hell I survived," I gaped as we crossed the state line and reentered Michigan.

"Chip," Lisa began, as she shuffled through the stack of documents, "he was more brutal than I ever could've imagined. It is fate that you are still alive."

"It just didn't sink in until . . . oh my God," I said in a slow, measured tone.

"What is it?" asked Lisa, quickly raising her head to look out the window.

"No," I said, tightening my grip on the steering wheel, "not outside. The newspaper articles—when did it say the murder occurred?"

Lisa flipped through the paperwork and found the copy of the newspaper clipping.

"Here it is. August first, 1970. Wh—"

Her eyes confirmed my own feeling of bewilderment.

"My birthday—five years to the day."

Knowing how superstitious Leslie and Michael were, there was no way that date could be a coincidence. The chances of Michael Grant murdering a child and then coincidentally becoming a father on the exact same day five years later were nearly impossible. This clue implied that something far more sinister might have taken place.

⌐━━◆━━⌐

Even with the new information, I found it extremely difficult to make sense of it all. I felt like I was falling into a gaping
chasm, with clues that led nowhere. I had plenty of theories,
plenty of speculations, yet nothing could be confirmed. I was
emotionally drained and anxious. I was exhausted, yet could
barely sleep when I lay down at night. Even when my head hit
the pillow, the memories and nagging questions kept gnawing
at me.

*This is a prescription for Paxil. It will help with your anxiety,*
the doctor stated through a thick, Middle-eastern accent.

*I need this?* I asked.

*After what you've told me you've been through, I believe you do.
I'm prescribing Xanax, too,* he added.

*How long do I have to stay on these medications?*

*You can stay on them as long as you need to. Some people stay on
them their entire lives. Don't worry, this will help* . . .

After a few weeks, I felt a bit calmer and less anxious, but I
still needed answers. I don't think all the medications in the
world could have suppressed my desire for the truth.

I decided to have another conversation with Leslie. I learned
that she was on probation from the embezzlement charges and
was currently working in an auto-parts factory. She was dating
one of her coworkers, although I had serious doubts that she had
severed her ties with Michael Grant. I hoped that under different circumstances, she would be more willing to offer the truth.

Leslie agreed to meet us in an open park, not far from the
apartment community she once managed. We waited at an old,

dilapidated picnic table, letting the distant sunlight warm our faces on that cool, autumn morning. I was enveloped in thought and filled with questions when I noticed a figure approaching from the grassy field beyond.

"Hello, Leslie," I said as she reached the table.

I no longer felt comfortable referring to either one of them as "Mom" or "Dad"—not only because the evidence seemed to suggest otherwise, but also because they didn't earn the titles. Biologically or not, a parent needs to value the privilege of being so and live up to the name.

"Hi," she answered coldly. "Boy, I sure hope you guys aren't bugged."

Lisa and I exchanged glances as Leslie anxiously scanned the park. I pulled out a prepared list of questions and began firing them at her, one by one. She casually fielded each with a simple "yes" or "no," causing me growing frustration.

"You can add more if you think of anything," I offered sarcastically.

"Okay."

"How many abortions have you had?" I asked, alluding to the letters I discovered in the trunk.

"Oh, uh," she stammered, "about four or five."

"Did Michael ever try to kill me?"

"Well," she began uncomfortably, "not really. No. No, he didn't."

"Did you kill Beau? I won't hold it against you. I know you were under a lot of stress," I lied.

"Well, I guess so. I had just gotten a really shitty letter from Mike. He was angry I wasn't helping him get out of prison faster. I got so upset . . ."

*She's no different from Michael Grant,* I thought.

The meeting didn't yield any new leads, but it did confirm one thing: Leslie was dangerous. If cornered, she would steal, con, or even kill.

# CHAPTER
# 13

# Gentle Rain

THE BEDROOM WAS BLACK as a pit, silvery-blue moonlight playing upon shapes outside the open doorway. A force, almost magnetic, drew me from beneath the heavy comforter to the moonlit room beyond. As I glided out of the room, I glanced back to see Lisa's silhouette, vaguely outlined by the bay window, still as death. I could scarcely breathe upon entering the living room and caught notice of the bewitching moon cast in the sky through a clouded picture window. Its color was neither yellow nor silver, but a horrid blood red, as a stain upon the night sky.

I opened my mouth to call out, but voiceless I remained, steadily traveling onward through the house at a swift clip. The room was abnormally large and overwhelming, and suddenly my pace seemed to dwindle to that of oozing molasses. Protest as I might, my feet kept the slow, unnatural rhythm through the living room toward the dining area.

I could barely make out a figure standing in the adjoining kitchen when a terrible bellow rose in the air. The mysterious, menacing figure lurched forward suddenly, letting out a hoarse moan. I held my course to dare a look at its face.

*My father . . .*

He darted in my direction. My arms did not respond, nor did my legs. Tears streamed down my face as he approached me, the look of the devil himself emblazoned in his eyes.

"Help me!" I cried. "Lisa, help me!"

"Chip! Chip! It's okay, honey," came a soothing voice from somewhere outside the darkness. "Wake up, Chip. It's me. I'm here. You're okay!"

"Oh, God," I mumbled, rolling over into Lisa's arms. "I couldn't move. It was so dark."

"It's okay," she whispered gently. "You're okay now."

*Imagine,* I thought, *if I were going through this, walking this path without her.*

*Alone.*

Lisa and I had been experiencing one calamity after another for so long that I never really considered the sacrifices and challenges *she* was facing. Our relationship had been anything but easy from the very beginning. Yet something divine held Lisa faithfully by my side. Through all the hurt and angst, Lisa gave her love effortlessly and endlessly. I had chosen Michael Grant over her hundreds of times. And in the end, when hell battered me with the worst of its fury, Lisa was there. Through it all, she was my friend, my lover, my confidante, my soul mate. She could have easily chosen another man who was free of the enormous baggage I carried.

But there she was, searching through that mysterious black trunk, over and over, trying to help me find my identity. Suddenly, my focus shifted; my perspective changed.

"It doesn't matter," I said softly one morning as I lowered the lid. "Come with me."

We left our apartment and drove through the streets lined with newly painted autumn leaves. The glorious colors reached deep within my heart and made me feel alive again. Somewhere along the way I had forgotten how beautiful nature could be. Somehow I had let the darkness creep inside me, casting a shadow on all that was good and bright in the world.

Having reached our destination, I turned the car off and stepped out. The soft, cool breeze brushed back my hair, and the smoky scent of burning leaves tickled my nose.

Lisa got out of the car and shut the door. "Where are we?"

"It's not far now," I said, taking her hand.

We passed alongside a row of bushes, which seemed much smaller than I had remembered. After weaving through a couple of buildings, we stumbled upon some children playing baseball in the street. They laughed without a worry or a care, leaving me with a familiar feeling of envy.

I led Lisa around another building and into a grassy field. Ahead stood the old, wooden gazebo. As we neared, I noticed that someone had sealed up the opening below the gazebo with latticework. I didn't plan on crawling beneath it this time because my sense of peace and solitude was walking beside me.

We walked up the worn, gray steps, and I ran my hand along the flaking, splintered pillar as I passed. Crossing the wooden floor to the built-in benches, I took both of Lisa's hands as we sat down.

"Lisa, you have remained by my side through things that defied comprehension. Writers often try to capture the love, the devotion, the compassion you've shown me in poems and stories, because it's so rare. You've shown me those qualities, but I've taken them for granted. You've put your entire life on hold to help me reconstruct mine. Whether we succeed doesn't matter. What does matter is that you tried . . . for me. I brought you here today because I wanted to share with you something very special to me. This is where I would run, to feel safe, when I was a child. This was my castle. Nobody ever knew what this place meant to me, but I wanted you to be a part of it. I wanted to make you a part of my past, and I want to make you a part of my future."

I slowly knelt down beside her and pulled out the small, black velvet box I had placed deep within my coat pocket only hours before.

"I may not know who I *was*, but I know who I *am*. I know who I want to be. I want to be your husband. Will you marry me?"

"Yes," she breathed, her eyes glistening.

Opening the box and removing the sparkling band, I gently slipped it onto Lisa's trembling finger.

"I love you," she whispered, embracing me.

And within her words I could almost feel the heat subsiding, the gentle drops of rain.

# Open Wounds

MINDFUL OF SECRETS THAT may lay beneath the black lid in the deep, old trunk, I packed it away in the back corner of a long closet and prepared to make a new life with Lisa—a better one.

Nearly one year after the only world I had ever known was ripped out from beneath me, we were making plans for the day soon to come when we would exchange vows and pledge our love to one another. We ultimately decided on Valentine's Day, the day that inspires passion and celebrates the greatest loves throughout the ages.

In the hectic weeks leading up to the wedding, Lisa and I found ourselves in the eye of a new storm of chaos. There were reservations to be made, contracts to be signed, and invitations to be sent. Yet the hurdles of cranky caterers and testy florists were nothing compared to the world we were gladly leaving behind.

But our bliss was short-lived. A dreaded early morning phone call shattered our serenity and stopped our hearts just six weeks before we were to be wed.

"Dad, what's wrong?" Lisa pleaded, stumbling to her feet in the darkened bedroom.

"Mom died last night . . ." her father sobbed.

Lisa's mother, Karen, had been in failing health for several years. She had a history of medical problems and had been scheduled for one surgery after another. Recently, the doctors had removed a lithe lodged in her lung and given her a good prognosis for recovery. Apparently, her health had taken a sudden turn for the worse, and she had suffered a massive heart attack at the age of only forty-nine.

The loss of her mother was a tremendous blow to Lisa. While her heart certainly wasn't into the wedding, we had no choice but to proceed. Contracts had been signed, deposits had been made, and invitations had been sent. We slowly and steadily counted the days until the bittersweet occasion.

Then, one chilly winter morning just weeks before our wedding, I ripped open a letter I found in our frosted mailbox, and with it an old, throbbing wound. "Indiana State Prison" was the return address.

"Lisa!" I shouted frantically as I tore into our apartment. "You'll never believe this! Michael Grant has been granted parole!"

According to the letter, Michael Grant was eligible for parole because he had no record of bad behavior while in society for the past twenty-six years. Indiana wasn't pursuing the escape charges and most likely would release him within the month, barring any further information or testimony to the contrary.

"I have to write them. They have to know," I said to Lisa.

"You've told me some of the things your fath—, he did to you. There's more, isn't there?" Lisa asked softly.

All I could do was nod and choke back tears. I still had not revealed to Lisa all the horrors I had endured, the scars buried deep within my mind. Some I was too ashamed to speak of, others I had locked away. There were memories I vowed never to visit again, yet now I was being called on to do so.

She brought a hand to my cheek. "It's going to be hard, but I'm here."

"I have to do it or I'm no better than Leslie. Or Aunt Chris or anyone else who knew this awful secret."

I immediately set to drafting a letter, crumpling up page after page until our living room floor was adorned with crisp, white, paper snowballs. As I sat on the couch, I read and reread the fin- ished product until I was satisfied, then drove with Lisa to the post office to send it certified mail.

I called two days later to check the tracking number and make certain my letter had been received. The post office con- firmed receipt, but Lisa suggested that we not take any chances.

"Why don't you call the prison to be sure?"

"You think I need to?"

"Don't you think we should make sure? Just to verify it's in the right hands."

"You're right," I said, reaching for the phone.

"Indiana State Prison," announced a voice on the other end.

"I need to check on the status of a letter I sent to the parole board."

"Who is the offender?"

"Michael Grant, number 37670."

"Are you a relative?"

"I'm . . . he's my father."

"All I show is he's been granted parole. There is no hearing scheduled."

"Can you verify the address?" I said, feeling a little panicked.

In a flurry of questions tossed back and forth, I verified all the information. The prison had no record of the letter.

"I'm sending it again," I told Lisa after hanging up.

An hour later another certified letter was in the mail and Indiana bound. When tracking confirmed that the letter was received two days later, I was back on the phone with the prison. After several transfers I was connected to an aide to the parole board.

"Your letters have been received, Mr. St. Clair," she informed me.

"Are you sure? I was told by someone else that there's no record of my letters."

"I've read them."

"You—you have?" I began. "Is the board going to have a hearing?"

"Your letters aren't being taken very seriously. Grant has already been given parole. Once those wheels are in motion, the board typically doesn't like to shift gears. He's befriended many people here, including staff members. He lied and said he's in for killing a guy in a bar fight, not child murder. Child murderers and child molesters are on the lowest rung in the prison hierarchy. He tries to play real nice and friendly, but I've seen him snap. He doesn't fool me. Doesn't like me either. He knows I see through him."

"What can I do?"

"If you can't make them read your letter, then maybe you should come here and make them listen. I can set up a public hearing for you."

"Lisa," I breathed after hanging up, "the letter isn't going to be enough. It looks like we're going to have to go to Indiana."

I looked upon the parole board members, exhausted, drained, yet in muted exhilaration because I had engaged and survived the battle all of us must fight: the one within. That day, in my testimony before the parole board, I had come out victorious no matter what their decision. For that reason, this day belonged to me. Even so, I knew that the fate of Michael Grant rested in their hands, and as I rose from my chair, I couldn't help but wonder if what I shared with them would have any impact at all.

"Thank you for your testimony," said the head of the parole board, nodding politely. "You will be notified of our decision shortly."

As I pushed in the chair and turned around, his voice took on an icy tone.

"You know he'll be released eventually. I mean, we can't keep him here forever."

I stopped and turned to face Mr. Penfold.

"Nearly all the inmates in this prison will be released eventually. Why not just let them all out now?" I asked sharply. "I'm sorry to have wasted your time. And mine."

"I assure you, Mr. St. Clair," said one of the younger members in a sympathetic tone, "your time was not wasted here."

My mind spun wildly as we drove back home that February afternoon. The sky was a blank canvas, the road was never-ending. I thought of my life as that long road, stretching out infinitely to new possibilities. My rearview mirror reflected the road I was leaving behind: the haunting memories and unanswered questions. I knew that someday in the quest for my identity I would have to turn around and search the road for more clues, more pieces to the puzzle. But I could only go in one direction at a time—forward or back, the future or the past. By uncovering Michael Grant's true identity, I lost my own. But as I reached out and clasped Lisa's hand in mine, her bright smile reminded me of who I was and who I was soon to become. In a few days, I would become Lisa's husband, keeping my eyes firmly on the road ahead.

# CHAPTER 15

# Shrouded in Darkness

Look WHAT A BEAUTIFUL day it is!"

"Yeah," I breathed from behind closed eyelids in a failed attempt to mirror Lisa's enthusiasm.

Despite learning that we had been successful—that Michael Grant's parole had been rescinded and he wouldn't be due for another parole hearing for several years—a torrent of emotion swirled within me.

Lisa remained every bit as loving and compassionate as the day I married her. But I continued to feel a void—an overwhelming emptiness, like a sailing ship lost at sea when the wind turns suddenly and dies out.

I leaned forward and caught the bright sunlight that diffused through the airy curtains of our bedroom bay window. Although

we had lived in our new home for nearly two years, I still occasionally found myself confused upon waking, not remembering
the room I was in. Perhaps it stemmed from nearly thirty moves
throughout my life. While I was trying to move on with my new
life, something inside me remained uneasy.

"We're gonna have a great day today!" Lisa exclaimed
cheerfully.

"What's on the agenda?" I asked, flopping my head back to
my pillow.

"Well, I was thinking we could do a little spring cleaning.
Maybe organize the closets . . ."

"Ugh," I moaned, rolling onto my side.

". . . and maybe a little gardening after breakfast," she added.

"Great," I murmured unenthusiastically, with my face buried
in the pillow.

"Oh, come on," Lisa sang, bouncing out of bed.

I staggered tiredly out of the bedroom, trailing behind her
toward the kitchen, when I suddenly sensed disarray.

"The pillows," I remarked excitedly, pointing to the sofa.
"They're all messed up."

Lisa looked from me, to the sofa, then back to me again.

"They're *throw* pillows. They're made to be used."

"I know, but it looks like a disaster!" I announced, fluffing
and patting the pillows, then stepping back to admire my
work.

"Come on, Chip. Just relax. Your da . . . Michael Grant isn't
here," Lisa said.

"But," I began in protest until Lisa took my hand. "I guess you're right. Let me just fix this—"

"No," Lisa said firmly, pulling me away. "Let's make some breakfast."

I crossed the cold tile floor and stopped before the tall maple cupboards. The clatter of the pans echoed from behind.

A small pill bottle rested eye-level at the front of the shelf. As I picked it up, I felt a trace of fear at how light it seemed.

"Only two doses left," I said, a bit too casually as I emptied the contents onto my palm.

I studied the two small pink pieces, just remnants of the original oval pill.

I had been on Paxil and Xanax for nearly two years. The anti-depressants helped some, I admit, but they made everything seem slightly out of focus; I lived in a comforting numbness. Never too happy or too sad—just a moderate range of average emotions—always remote from intensity. And I couldn't help but wonder each day that I depended on those pills to sleep and relax, if I was walking down the same path as my father.

So I had decided to slowly wean myself off the prescriptions. And with the weaning came the side effects, including anxiety about not having anxiety medications.

I glanced over to catch Lisa purse her lips into a smile. She cracked an egg into a glass bowl.

"You'll be fine, Chip. You've already cut down to a quarter-dose a day as it is."

Almost on cue, my stomach lurched. My head felt like an

iron veil was falling over it with a heavy, nauseating pressure. I slammed down the broken tablets and darted to the small bathroom in the hall. My body reeled with dry heaves as I hovered over the open porcelain bowl. Finally the withdrawal episode subsided.

Falling back against the wall, I took in slow, shallow breaths, trying to regain my strength.

"You okay, honey?" Lisa asked, rushing to my side.

"Yeah, I just feel weak," I said, adding coyly, "don't know if I'll be able to garden today."

"Oh, you!" Lisa laughed, helping me to my feet. "Have a seat and I'll get breakfast."

Morning light streamed into the house as we ate in comfortable silence, but something deep within me still felt cold. After breakfast we slipped into tattered tennis shoes and stepped outside, met by the blinding sun rising in the east.

"I think I'll work in the back," I squinted. "The sun's too bright on this side."

"Sounds good. There are some gloves in the garage."

I found the gloves and rounded the house toward the shaded backyard.

*Why do I feel so uneasy?* I wondered, while methodically plucking weeds from the flower beds.

*I feel so lost . . . and very small.*

I was surrounded by peace and beauty, both the nature around me and the love and devotion of Lisa, yet something silent, dark, and looming had seized my sense of freedom and held it captive. I thought of the black trunk tucked away in the spare bedroom closet. True, mysteries lurked, but that wasn't what seemed to be gnawing at my mind. This was an aching from my heart, something I couldn't quite put my finger on.

I remembered the dark waters of Lake Michigan. So cold, so alone.

*I feel like I'm drowning . . .*

"Aaah!"

A touch on my shoulder made me leap into the air and yell out in fright.

"It's me," Lisa began, "I—"

"Don't ever do that!" I snapped. "You know I can't stand to have someone creep up behind me. You scared me to death!"

"I'm sorry, Chip," Lisa said, looking down.

"Just be careful," I said, taking a deep breath. I saw genuine hurt in her sea-blue eyes. "It's okay. Sorry I snapped."

"I finished out front and just wondered if you wanted to take a break inside."

"Sure."

"Chip," Lisa asked hesitantly while strolling to the front door, "he did that a lot, didn't he? Sneak up on you and scare you, I mean."

"Yeah," I said, closing my eyes against the sun and the glare of my memories. "He would hide in my closet, or sometimes under my bed . . . and wait for me to fall asleep."

"Oh, Chip," Lisa said, taking my hand.

"I would wake to hear this groaning sound growing louder,"

I began with tears welling in my eyes, "and I'd jump from my bed, and this hand, this hand would grab me. It would grab my foot and pull me under the bed."

Gritting my teeth, I sank down onto the porch.

"I fought and screamed. I didn't know what the hell had me. I got scared every time. And I cried every time. Cried like a baby."

Lisa sat speechless, placing her arm over my shoulder.

"Like a baby," I repeated, angrily wiping the tears that fell across my face, "like now."

"You had a right to feel afraid. To cry," she consoled. "You have a right to cry now. It's okay."

"No." I shook my head. "I'm weak for crying."

"He wouldn't let you cry. You were never allowed to deal with your feelings the right way."

"That was a long time ago," I said, getting to my feet. "It doesn't matter now."

"I remember reading somewhere that the tears we cry when we are upset are actually different in chemical makeup from tears from allergies and things like that. When we cry, I guess toxins are released. And so when you hold it in, you are really hurting yourself . . ."

"Can't we talk about something else? Let's get started on spring cleaning, okay?" I suggested firmly.

"Okay," Lisa said softly, following me inside.

I felt so heavy, so tired. Like I was sinking. . . .

Despite having moved into our house nearly two years before, there were many boxes we had not yet sorted. Perhaps it's human nature—unpacking what you need at the moment and saving the rest for later. The bottom of the priority list was uncovered as Lisa scavenged through plastic crates full of memorabilia in the walk-in closet.

"Ooh," she gasped and snatched off the lid.

Plopping down for a trip down memory lane, Lisa called me over to share her findings.

"This was an award I received in orchestra," she beamed. "And this is a project I worked on for weeks."

Emerging from the crate was a large, laminated poster board bound by metal rings. The word "leaves" was spelled out in an intricate pattern of tiny, elliptical leaves.

"This is great," I commented, kneeling down beside her.

As I flipped through the pages, studying the various leaves collected from all over the county, Lisa plucked more memories from the clear plastic crate.

"And this was a part of my Brownie uniform. And—"

"Brownie?" I inquired, lowering the leaf project to the floor.

"Yeah, it's like Girl Scouts. And here is . . ."

Her voice faded while I inspected the crate myself, a little curious about what was inside.

A bluish-gray paper was rolled and stuffed along the edge, barely noticeable.

I slid it out slowly and suddenly recognized what I held. Turning away from Lisa, I unrolled the paper and revealed the chalky, black charcoal of my self-portrait, the vacant eyes staring back at me. A lifeless stare.

"What's that?" she asked, craning her neck to see what I was holding.

"Oh, nothing. Just garbage. Something I should have thrown out long ago," I said casually, casting it errantly to the side.

Seeming unsatisfied with my answer, Lisa crawled over to retrieve it.

"Wow," she said upon unfurling it. "This is amazing! A self-portrait. When did you do this?"

"In high school," I said uncomfortably.

"Why don't you want to keep it?"

"It's . . . it's just junk. It's not even finished anyway."

"But still . . ."

"Just throw it away."

"No way. I'm going to keep it. Look at how crumpled it is. We should—"

"No!" I flared, jerking it from her hand. "Just throw it out. I should have left it in the trash."

"Chip . . ."

"It's shit!" I screamed, flashing Lisa an icy glare. Scooping up the portrait, I chucked it from the closet into the den. Lisa stood up and tried to slip past me, but I threw my body into the doorway and grabbed her by the arms with a fierce squeeze. The once serene pools of blue in her eyes shifted to dark, unsettled waters—a brooding, mighty storm.

"Get your hands off me," she warned, leveling her eyes to me. "You are not Michael Grant, and I'll be damned if I'll stand here and let you turn into him."

Her words pierced me deep, cutting clear to my soul. I eased my hold and stared in amazement. I had never seen Lisa—or any other woman in my life—act like that. So strong. Her eyes relaxed a little as I watched her resume her mission to retrieve the portrait.

"I—I don't know what happened to me. I'm sorry," I whispered, feeling myself sinking.

"What is happening to you?" she asked, unrolling the bluish-gray paper.

"I don't know."

"I think I do. It's them. What they did to you. You have nightmares constantly. You wake up drenched in sweat. I see you fluffing pillows, walking around vacuum lines, organizing anything and everything."

"I . . ." I tried to protest.

"No, listen. I love you. I want to help you. For God's sake, Chip, you can't even sit for two minutes without finding something to occupy your mind."

"Because if you had in your head what I do, you wouldn't want any free time to remember it!" I cried.

"What?" Lisa approached, putting a soothing hand to my forehead. "What do you have locked in here?"

"I . . ."

"You've got to talk to me. You've got to open up, to let out what's inside you. If you bottle it up, it will kill you. It already is."

"Do you," I sobbed, "do you think I'm like him? Do you think I'm destined to be like him?"

I sank to the floor and let go, crying uncontrollably.

What was it in my father's past that made him destroy everything in his path? What made him want to consume all and control all? There was a foul poison coursing through his veins that warped his conscience so completely that he no longer searched for an antidote. Ultimately, if nothing existed to heal him, was I, too, destined never to heal?

"I put up walls to protect myself as a child. Brick by brick, I built a wall around myself so I would never hurt again. I locked doors in my mind that I can't go back to."

"Yes, you can," Lisa smiled softly, "with me. You don't have to reach into your mind alone anymore. You'll have me with you. We'll open those dark parts of your memory together, and we'll close the doors together one at a time. You don't have to be afraid anymore. You don't have to feel shame or guilt with me."

"I don't know . . . I don't know if I can," I shuddered while Lisa held me in her arms.

"I promise you can trust me. They undermined your ability to trust anyone, but I promise, I won't let you down. You have to believe in me. We're going to sort out the old memories and make new ones."

She pulled away and once again unrolled the portrait.

"I'm going to frame this—because *you* did it, and I love you."

"There is so much that happened, that causes me to ache deep down . . ."

"That's okay. You tell me when you're ready. Just remember I'm here. I'll always be here."

The night released the faint glow of a crescent moon as I lay in bed wrestling with what she had said. The ways I behaved, the ways I felt, and the thoughts I had were all based upon my parents.

To truly discover who I was, I needed to be honest about my feelings. For that I would need to trust in someone outside the walls I had carefully constructed around me. Brick by brick, I needed to tear down the walls I had fought so long to keep in place.

"Lisa?" I whispered in the still night.

"Mmmm," she mumbled, deep in slumber.

"Lisa? I need to talk."

"O-okay," she breathed heavily, sitting up. "I'm here."

Bricks began to fall that evening, and with them many tears from me and from Lisa. Hours passed while we held each other and talked, until suddenly a glorious dawn broke—an eastern sun that dispelled the harsh darkness and kissed new life into all it touched.

# CHAPTER
# 16

# The Butterfly
# Garden

REALITY RARELY CHANGES; only our perspective of it. The means to change our surroundings depends on our own ability to shift perspectives. And that ability demands two prerequisites: desire and commitment. I had marshaled both to battle the demons inside me, the demons that eventually consumed my father. His childhood was less than remarkable from stories I had heard. Yet he allowed wretched shadows to enter his heart and overpower him with hate, anger, and fear. He joined the ranks of those demons, devouring and consuming his surroundings until nothing but destruction was left in his wake. I could sense those same demons in me; the fear, anger, and the hate that were only tenuously held at bay by the smoldering embers of hope I had found in literature as a child, and again in the glowing sunrise of Lisa's love for me. Now I knew that my father's chosen path into the abyss would not be the path I would tread. I would choose a different way.

Lisa was now walking beside me, helping me unlock the dark memories that lurked in the recesses of my mind. She brought light to my soul with the things that I had abandoned long ago: poetry, music, and nature.

"Chip, you're not focusing," Lisa said, shaking me from a deep trance.

"Sorry. Where was I?" I asked, studying the sheet music.

"Here," Lisa pointed at a cluster of black notes.

"Right," I said, positioning my fingers on the corresponding black and white keys of the piano.

The melancholy tune wafted into the air. It was not quite the way Beethoven intended *Moonlight Sonata* to sound, I'm certain, but I took great pride and pleasure in hearing it nonetheless. Lisa's family had owned a piano during her childhood. After years of lessons, she had had to suspend her passion for the instrument when her family was forced to sell it prior to an out-of-state move. When the opportunity arose for us to purchase one, I made a deal with her.

*You have to teach me Beethoven's* Moonlight Sonata.

*You have to learn the scales first,* she laughed. *And lessons! You'll need to start with beginners' books and . . .*

*Please teach me this first.*

I eventually conceded to learning the basic scales and how to read notes. Then, one note at a time, Lisa began her instruction as promised. She knew what the song meant to me in relation to my attempted suicide. She knew what it meant for me to learn it. She was helping me open another door.

"Good. Very good," she exclaimed. "It's sounding much more graceful. Make sure you let off the foot pedal. That's right."

My fingers were stiff and clumsy, my pace slow, but I played the song through to the end.

"Wonderful! Why don't we call it a day and go for a drive? It's a beautiful morning. Maybe we can go on a picnic."

"That would be great," I said, smiling.

Lisa knew I had never gone on picnics as a child, and lately we were enjoying frequent outings as she helped me make new memories.

We threw together a basket of sandwiches, munchies, and lemonade, tossed them into the back of our Mustang, and set off for the nearest green glade under a cloudless blue sky.

Our favorite park was empty except for a couple of joggers engrossed in their exercise routines. There we planted ourselves near a small lake under a great oak with branches outstretched, raising its arms to the sun as if in reverence to nature's beauty.

Upon eating my fill, I fell backward next to Lisa and stared up at the sky through the trees. I closed my eyes to listen to the birds serenading us.

"Are your shoes still on?" she scolded playfully.

"Oh, yeah." I sat up swiftly and began untying them. "I almost forgot."

I lay back down, absorbing the feeling of cool blades of grass against my bare feet.

We rested in silence for awhile. I may have even drifted off to sleep when Lisa cried out suddenly.

"Hey! I know where we should go. Come on."

The air turned thick and humid when we passed through the solid glass doors to the room beyond. Bright sunlight slipped through a vaulted glass dome above and dappled the enclosure with soft touches of glowing warmth.

"You've never been here before?" Lisa asked.

I shook my head, enchanted by the sanctuary we had entered. Exotic greenery lined winding paths, and we found ourselves surrounded by colorful gardens encased by stone. A trellis overflowed with vines and flowers that spilled over a pathway and down to a bench below. The sounds of flowing water rained from a fountain, falling droplets dancing on the pond's surface. And among the intricately woven labyrinth of paths, visitors dotted this oasis of beauty, paying silent homage to a place that captivated all the senses.

As I looked around, something even more wondrous captured my attention—something that would leave a lasting impression and ultimately change my life forever. Floating effortlessly among the visitors, gliding from flower to flower, was a myriad of butterflies. In a dazzling bouquet of colors, they simultaneously exhibited their agility and exposed their vulnerability, fluttering among those who could easily do them harm yet were transfixed in awe and amazement.

"A butterfly garden," I said, scarcely breathing.

Lisa smiled, taking my hand and leading me to a stone bench that bordered the small pond. Glistening coins carpeted the water's bottom, reflecting the wishes made upon them.

From there I watched an iridescent blue butterfly with black edges on its wings sail past and land on a nearby flower. I moved in as close as I dared to study it unrolling a long, thin tube to draw out the flower's nectar. Its colors were stunning, almost like minute fish scales blended together in a shimmering brilliance of blue and silver.

From the corner of my eye, I noticed a broad, burly man wearing rugged blue jeans, a grungy T-shirt, and black motorcycle boots. A dark-blue bandanna was wrapped tightly around what seemed to be a clean-shaven head. His face had not seen the sharp side of a razor in days.

I fought the urge to back away as he came closer, his hardened expression softening to a smile when he noticed the butterfly. He leaned in, his smile widening in succession with his eyes, as he studied the butterfly I had been observing. For a moment I could picture him as a child, staring with wonder and innocence. As the butterfly flitted away, his gaze followed, still reflecting some forgotten bliss; but, as he turned to meet my gaze, his hardened expression returned.

I turned to Lisa sitting beside me, curious to see if she had witnessed what had just happened. She was watching a small yellow butterfly fold and unfold its wings on the outstretched arm of a little girl. The child smiled and stole a glance at her mother, who stroked her light brown hair with a laugh.

"This place . . . is amazing," I whispered.

Lisa broke her stare to offer a smile and then returned her attention to the little girl.

I sighed and leaned back on my palms, gazing up toward the glass dome, butterflies of all sorts of shapes and colors swirling in a gentle whirlwind.

*From a caterpillar to this,* I thought. *What a transformation.*

And with that thought, an enormous floodgate burst open, releasing the swelling waters of understanding. I scrambled to search my mind for anything I knew about caterpillars and butterflies.

From what I remembered in school, a caterpillar hatches from an egg with a single mission: to eat, to devour everything in its path. In a feeding frenzy, it searches its surroundings, and when it has finally gotten its fill, it builds a cocoon. There, in that secluded space, it wraps itself away from the world to complete its life cycle by making a magnificent transformation. Soon a delicate butterfly emerges, drying its damp wings in the heat of the sun. From that moment on, the butterfly has a new mission, a new path in life: to pollinate and to spread beauty in the world one flower at a time. In doing so, it offers that beauty to anyone fortunate enough to savor the simple pleasure of basking in its radiance.

*To make the world more beautiful,* I thought.
*Caterpillars consume, devour, feed . . .*
*Like my father . . .*

The earthbound caterpillar devours all that surrounds it in its environment, and in many species, what it has consumed determines its colors—its ultimate form—when it becomes a butterfly. Through a unique process, the particular plants the caterpillar eats are metabolized and stored, then finally reflected in the colors of its wings after its metamorphosis. If the caterpillar consumes exotic plants, those plants metabolize into exotic colors when the butterfly emerges from the cocoon. Some species of caterpillars devour toxic plants and metabolize them into toxic chemicals that are expressed in various color patterns upon their wings as butterflies—subsequently posing warnings to potential predators. Each butterfly's wings are unique in appearance because each butterfly encountered different circumstances as a caterpillar. The fuel of its past provides the strength to transform itself into something beautiful, something distinctive, reflecting the colors within.

We human beings, too, have a path in life, and our experiences—both good and bad—are to be used as tools to forge onward. If we don't use the tools we are given, does that not violate nature's design? Are those who choose to consume and destroy their environment—instead of re-creating themselves in a loftier form—akin to the lowly, earthbound caterpillar? Are those who fail to master their demons, who never digest and

transform the experiences of the past, destined to remain caterpillars, crawling through life for the rest of their days?

*People like my father.*

But to build a cocoon! To seal ourselves away from this world
in a silent space of introspection. Alone, the caterpillar builds its
private sanctuary, and alone it must remain, drawing on the past
for the strength to make its transformation into something
spectacular.

To give ourselves over to introspection is to build our own
private cocoon. Just as nothing can help the caterpillar while it
undergoes its transformation, no one can assist us in the process
of self-examination or assess the depth of our commitment to
the path of change. At that moment, sitting on the stone bench,
I realized that the answers I needed to achieve peace and understanding had been inside me all along.

*Lisa can be here for support, but the metamorphosis must come
from within.*

I felt my eyes filling with tears as I watched the gentle butterflies soar high above. I closed my eyes and imagined myself rising
up, free and light, dancing among them, the sun warming my soul.

*I want to soar.*

To emerge free. Just as the butterfly's purpose is to emerge
from a cocoon and soar, we, too, must bring forth our colors
from within, not hide them from the world—for they are part of
our very being, the palette of our life's experiences. We must not
be afraid to reveal the rainbow buried deep within us, to spread
our wings and help make the world flourish.

I looked over to find Lisa smiling at me.

"This place," I said softly, "this represents what the world is: a butterfly garden."

I slipped my arm around her as she settled her head upon my shoulder, both of us tucked away in the hidden tranquility.

And suddenly, in the bright light of my epiphany, the darkness lifted. At that moment, I knew that my own personal metamorphosis had begun. And as I held her in my arms, I realized something else: Lisa had been a butterfly from the moment I laid eyes on her.

# CHAPTER 17

# Mastering Demons

Flames leapt wildly within the fireplace, and as crisp, crackling sounds filled the living room, I couldn't help but feel a serenity within the orange blaze. Even within chaos there can remain a steadfast peace, a predictability. The demons dancing in the brickwork were raging, yet contained, just as the demons that dwelled inside me were now tempered by my newfound insight. I understood that even *they* had a purpose, not in fueling my fear, but in fueling my passion to soar. And sometimes passion cannot be ignited without a spark.

The weeks leading up to this cool, autumn evening were filled with self-examination. I had built my cocoon—analyzing certain aspects of my life, my memories fond and harsh—and embraced them *all*.

Through introspection I finally understood that events beyond our control deal us the hand we get to play in life. Everything we experience shapes us, including the experiences that cause us pain. And what may still haunt us today are merely the shadows of the demons of yesterday. By embracing the shadows of my past, I began to master my demons. In the newfound light of peace and hope for the future that radiated from within me, I could begin to illuminate the recesses of my mind that were once shrouded in darkness.

While I absorbed the heat from the fire, Lisa asked me to open another door in my mind, one I had closed and locked tight with everything else in my past.

"Why don't you write some poetry?"

"What?" I asked, a little startled. "Now?"

"Why not? You look so peaceful sitting there."

"I can't tell you how long it's been since I wrote anything."

"I know," Lisa nodded, rising from the sofa. "But why don't you just try? Here, I'll get some paper."

A moment later she returned from the kitchen with a tablet and a pen.

"Just write how you feel," she added.

The paper was blank and glaring and remained that way for so long that I thought my creativity was a neglected well run dry.

And then it happened. My pen touched the paper, and ink began to flow. My spidery scribbling filled the page, and I hastily flipped to the next. And the next. And the next.

My hand was cramping, yet I continued to write. Poems,

verses, thoughts, quotes, anything and everything overflowed onto the paper like a dam that had burst, flooding the room with emotion. The fire had since died out, and Lisa's body now rose and fell in the rhythm of sleep, but I continued to write long into the night.

The black ink that drained from my pen may well have been a needle drawing life's blood from my arm and injecting it into the paper, for that is how I felt, writing.

Eventually, sleep beckoned me to stop the frenzied rush of passionate scribbling, and I fell under its spell, nodding off.

I awoke the next morning to find that the most wonderful dream I'd been dreaming wasn't that at all, for I lay among scores of unbound leaves, each filled with a part of me.

In no time I was back at it, having enlisted the soft elegance of Vivaldi's *Four Seasons* as background music for inspiration. I wrote about fate in a poem I titled "Knight Eternal." I wrote about love in "I Hear Her Whisper in the Rain." I wrote about inspiration in "Basking in the Moonlight."

"Now *you're* inspiring me to play the piano," Lisa chuckled when I stopped to massage my aching hand.

"Then play for me," I laughed.

Lisa's sea-blue eyes glistened as she spun around, her long dark hair sweeping in an arc behind her.

"And you can write for me."

"Lisa?" I called as she turned to walk into the piano room.

"Yeah?" she paused.

"Thank you . . . for everything."

She leaned back and blessed me with one of the most beautiful smiles I'd ever seen.

With all due respect to Vivaldi, hearing the one you love serenade you touches the deepest reaches of your soul. Her fingers floated across the keys in unrivaled grace. I leaned my head back and listened to the passion playing upon the keys and imagined Lisa all alone on a tropical island with nothing to do but play the piano at the water's edge on a white, sanded shore.

I picked up my pen and transcribed what I saw in my mind's eye—Lisa playing against the power of nature without a care in the world.

When the music had ceased and Lisa had left the still room, I called to her.

"Lisa, come here."

"What is it?"

"Come sit next to me."

She settled in beside me and spotted the title of the poem I had written.

"So Grand," she announced, then continued to read aloud:

> *Set my soul to a vast, empty sea,*
> *Writing letters to no one in sand;*
> *Yet voiceless, downtrodden, and lonely I'd be*
> *If not for a piano so grand.*
>
> *For in the air of my island home*
> *I'd fill with my new voice in key;*

*'Til day wakens night, 'til feet felt by foam,*
*Traversing the world by symphony.*

*And let the silence be broken by the swing of my staff,*
*Let the stars measure twinkle in time;*
*While the rain and the wind command silence I laugh*
*And join in with rhythm and rhyme.*

*Ne'er needing food nor drink as I feast on the sound,*
*My music bringing harmony o'er the land;*
*Dreading the day when hence I am found*
*And swept from my piano so grand.*

An awkward silence followed the final words, making me a bit anxious, for I hadn't written for myself or anyone else in what seemed to be ages. Lisa knew, however, what it meant for me to transfer thought onto paper. She knew I wrote without fear, but with pure jubilation as I gave life to my feelings.

She also must have seen the flicker of passion in my eyes, as it had been so many years before.

At last she spoke.

"Welcome back."

# CHAPTER
## 18

# Chasing
# Butterflies

As THE FEELING OF peace grew within me, my heart became lighter. For the first time in my life, I felt an openness I had never felt before—but it would soon be tested.

"Hello," began the voice on the other end of the line. "Is this Chip St. Clair?"

"Yes, it is."

"I'm an editor for the *Detroit Free Press*. I heard about your story, about the situation with your father, and I think it's remarkable. I feel it would be a very compelling story for our readers."

I glanced over to Lisa, switching my phone to the other ear.

"Would you be willing to speak with one of our reporters?"

"Yes, that would be fine."

Within the hour, the phone rang again.

"Hello, Chip. My name is Lori. I'm a reporter for the *Free Press*. My editor said he spoke with you and that it would be okay for us to talk."

The reporter and I talked for nearly an hour, as I sketched out the details of my childhood, the surprise of uncovering my father's true identity as a child murderer, and the mysteries in the black trunk. I found that I could speak about each subject with less pain, even some objectivity, as if I were floating high above myself looking down.

"I'd love to meet with you. Can you come to my office?" she asked during a pause.

"Sure. I have a lot of documents as well. Police reports, court records, and, of course, the other things I found in the trunk."

"Well, bring *everything* you have, if you don't mind. I want to see if maybe we can get to the bottom of some of this."

Lori scavenged through the contents of the old trunk at our first of many meetings, scribbling notes furiously as she went along. Lisa and I planted ourselves in her office and examined the montage of clues.

"Sometimes I feel like I'm trying to put a puzzle together in the dark. There are thousands of pieces and I'm not even sure what fits where, or if it even fits at all," I mumbled softly.

"All of this is unbelievable. This has to be one of the most incredible stories I've ever heard," she remarked, holding up the pale green birth certificate to examine it.

"And look at these children," she said, mulling over a small child's photo in each hand. "Chip, there is no doubt in my mind that these are different kids. The one in the brown shirt may be you, but this other child—he doesn't even have the same chin! And his hair is lighter!"

"Look at this one," I said, pointing to one photograph I found especially peculiar. "It says 'Chip' on the back and shows a toddler in a zippered jumpsuit standing in an open room."

"Yeah," she said, examining the photo, "what's so strange about that?"

"Behind the child, there's a portrait hanging on the wall—a portrait of an obviously older boy wearing a jersey, number 22."

"Okay," she said, crinkling her brow.

"So there's an older child in the portrait on the wall, and the toddler in the foreground. Now look at this," I said, handing her another worn photo.

"He's wearing the number 22 jersey," she observed.

"Flip it over."

"Chip," she read aloud, "it's you! But that would mean the toddler in the foreground, who is obviously younger, and the child in the portrait hanging on the wall are both you! That's impossible! How can an older child's portrait be on the wall of the house with the same younger child standing right in front of it? Unless one of them is not you . . ."

As the day wore on, we sorted through every detail stashed away in that old black trunk. Lori placed sticky notes on just about every picture, document, and folder, and had already begun categorizing them into possible theories. Before we left, she asked if there was any more information that we had not already given her, or anything else we knew about my past, or that of my parents'.

"After Michael Grant's arrest," I spoke solemnly, "we were trying to pick Leslie's brain. I needed answers. She told us we didn't know the half of it. She also rushed us outside and said she had things to burn. What you have is all that's left."

"I can't imagine what else there could be."

The story ran on December 17, 2002. From the moment I awoke that morning, I found I was holding my breath, as you would before taking a great plunge.

Lisa and I went about our daily routines, brushing our teeth, making breakfast, preparing for work. It all felt a bit surreal, knowing in the back of my mind that millions of readers would know the secrets I had locked away behind my eyes, the even darker secrets of the man I had called "Dad." Friends and neighbors whom I'd wave to, talk to, or help with their groceries—would their eyes reflect pity? Shame? Would they respect me?

"Are you ready?" I asked Lisa before hopping in the car.

"Yes," she said with a deep breath, knowing I was not speaking about work.

There was a gas station a few blocks from our house, and as

we approached I could see lines of cars waiting to fill up on that frosty morning. I parked near the front door and pulled out some change as I walked in.

Just inside the small building, under a long glass enclosure, were stacks of various papers. It didn't take long to spot the article because my face was smack in the middle of the front page. I picked up a copy as nonchalantly as possible, slipped the coins onto the counter, and returned to the car.

"It's on the front page?" Lisa said, awestruck, as I sat down and buckled my safety belt.

"Yeah. What does it say?"

Lisa read the article aloud as we drove to work. Soon the phone calls began. The first was from the *Free Press* reporter.

"I'm swamped with calls, Chip," she began excitedly. "People are calling to commend you for your strength. CNN just left a message."

"Really?" I exclaimed. "What do you think they want?"

"To interview you. Be prepared: You'll probably be getting a lot of calls."

That warning couldn't have been more prescient. Within hours I was speaking to producers at *Good Morning America* and *20/20*, and I had a list of other calls to return scratched on the back of an envelope.

Within days Lisa and I found ourselves on an airplane bound for New York, anxiously sorting documents for the producers of *Good Morning America*.

"Are you nervous?" Lisa asked as the FASTEN SEAT BELT sign lit up in anticipation of our descent.

"A little, I suppose."

But nerves quickly faded after three days in New York City. The taping seemed to sail by in the blink of an eye, and afterward I could hardly remember a thing I'd said. With the bright lights, the cameras, and the knowledge that millions would be watching, "overwhelming" was certainly an understatement.

Also overwhelming was the sense of relief we felt when our plane landed at Detroit Metro and we met the driver that *Good Morning America* had arranged to bring us home.

Lisa and I sat quietly in the back, each of us absorbed in our own thoughts, when suddenly the driver broke the silence.

"You have a nice trip?" he asked politely with a glance in the rearview mirror.

"Yes, it was fine," I smiled.

"Were you a guest on *Good Morning America*?"

"Yes," I nodded. "We taped yesterday but it won't air until next week, I guess."

"If you don't mind me asking, why were you on?"

"Well, it's kind of a long story. Maybe you saw the *Free Press* article a few days back?"

He shook his head while his gaze remained intently on me. I reiterated my story as he drove the bare highways, his eyes constantly shifting to the rearview mirror to make contact with mine. When I finished, he fixed his stare on the road, his jaw clenched. I studied him, wondering what he was thinking.

His head was rough stubble, his face worn with deep creases. I judged he could have been twice my age.

"My father," he said in a slow, measured tone, "was cruel. Not the same things you went through, but he was cruel."

"The pain we go through is relative. Pain is pain. I'm sorry for what happened to you."

"I—I never talk about it. My family, we get together, but we never talk about it. Good for you for being able to." Then he added, "I'll be watching for you. I won't forget."

The car jerked to a stop on the slanted driveway, and all of us got out. Lisa and I stretched wearily while the driver removed our luggage from the trunk and set it down near the garage.

"Thank you," he said, meeting my eyes before pulling the door shut.

When his car was out of sight, I turned to find Lisa collecting the black suitcases and bent down to help. Something leaning against the garage door caught my eye—a FedEx package carefully wrapped in clear plastic. The return address read *The John Walsh Show*.

"Looks like we're going back to New York," I remarked.

I admired John Walsh tremendously, for he had taken the absolutely horrific circumstances of the disappearance and murder of his son and transformed his pain into positive energy. So it was no great shock that I jumped at the opportunity when asked to share my story on his talk show, and finally meet the man I had grown to respect.

We ended up traveling to New York on several occasions for interviews, yet it was upon returning home that I began to realize the impact my story was making.

In my encounters in the weeks and months that followed, I found many people struggling with their own transformations. Some were beginning to soar; many were imprisoned in their own minds, guarded by demons of the past, but beginning to make a cocoon. . . .

*I saw you on TV,* one would say. *I was abused as a child, too.* . . .

*I never told anybody this, but my father raped me when I was twelve. From then on I started drinking and never stopped.* . . .

*My brother got in with the wrong crowd in high school. He started using drugs, and it eventually killed him. I feel so guilty that I couldn't help him.* . . .

*My grandma and I were very close. She was the only one I could count on. When I was nine, she was diagnosed with cancer, and I watched her deteriorate and die. I never got over it.* . . .

*I married a man just like my father. He broke my jaw before I had the strength to leave.* . . .

The conversations came while eating in restaurants, in the line at the grocery store, in busy shopping malls, even while washing my hands in the men's room. Complete strangers would approach me, often with swollen and teary eyes, and relive a horrible memory from their childhood or share a current hurdle in their life. Plagued with pain from a divorce, sexual abuse as a child or drug addiction, men and women from all walks of life were unearthing buried secrets and removing bricks from invisible walls they had built. They were confused and angry at how life had shortchanged them. They were asking why they were forced to endure such difficult circumstances; why they were cursed with such trials and tribulations.

Each time I was approached I felt an enormous renewal of strength and conviction. By allowing others a glimpse into the windows of my life, I was helping them reclaim something they believed had been lost in the storm that engulfed them. Something I found deep inside while struggling to survive in the dark, rolling waters of Lake Michigan: hope. Hope that lies within each of us—a hope that no one can hurt, that no darkness can touch.

At one point I met a teacher who felt that my message would benefit her fifth-grade class. She forewarned me that ten-year-olds have short attention spans; they might be disruptive or rude. She also suspected that many of them had problems at home, some yet to be identified by the school.

In my various media appearances, I briefly gave way to nervous jitters just before the interview; however, the sense of intimidation I felt before taping national news programs and speaking in front of live studio audiences paled in comparison to what I felt entering a classroom filled with thirty ten-year-olds. Suddenly I was ten years old again, small and frightened. I could almost picture myself cloaked in the shadows of the back of the class, feeling alone as I had so many years before. This was a door to the past that caught me unaware, but I soon took a deep breath and regained my composure.

"How many of you here like to read?" I began.

From the moment I asked that question to the chime of the bell signaling the end of school, time sailed by. We talked about books and fairy tales, and I subtly slipped in how literature provided a sanctuary for me as a child when I was hurting or felt alone. I shared a very watered-down rendition of the discovery of my father's true identity and briefly touched on the mysteries that remained. But the true focus of the discussion rested on my ability to overcome adversity and the strength that I believed existed within each one of them to overcome any obstacle life would throw their way. We talked about the things they liked to do, the things they were good at, and the things that made them happy. At the end of the class, I believe I walked away with more than I had given, for I saw in them the unconquerable courage and the bottomless fountain of hope that lie in the eyes of a child. Of all this world's beauty and miracles, brilliance and simplicity—of all nature's graces—children are truly the most remarkable.

Before Lisa and I left, a small boy with a head of brown curly hair approached me.

"I—I just wanted to say," he said from behind a quivering lip, "thank you."

He raised a trembling hand to me, and I gently grasped it with a smile.

"You're very welcome. Thank you."

The boy quickly stole his hand away and turned to leave. I studied him until he was out of sight. There was a great lump in my throat.

*That child was me,* I thought.

"Well, that's astounding!" the teacher gasped. "He hardly speaks to anyone. I wish I knew what was going on in his home. That child never opens up."

*Today he opened up,* I thought. *Perhaps someday he'll unfold his wings. . . .*

# CHAPTER 19

# Master of My Fate

I OFTEN THINK OF life as a great darkened room with a mammoth-sized tapestry fastened to a stone wall. All we have is the flicker of a candle's flame to catch glimpses of what the entire picture is to reveal, never quite able to see more than a little at a time. I believe true peace can be achieved not in viewing the whole tapestry, but in accepting without bitterness those portions we have been afforded the luxury to see. Yet sometimes circumstances arise that shed light on more than expected.

Some of the answers I had sought since *my* moment of truth in the stale bedroom of my parents were soon to be revealed.

Karen, an investigative reporter for a local TV news station, caught wind of my story and was determined to find answers. She examined clues, pored over documents, and pondered potential theories, as had those who came before her. But there was one avenue she was relentless in pursuing—one surefire way to resolve at least part of the puzzle.

"You know, Chip, a DNA test could determine whether they are truly your parents. I mean, we still wouldn't know about the other children in the pictures, or what other crimes they may have committed, but at least that mystery would be solved," she stated during one of our meetings.

In the past, the media had tracked them down for that very purpose. Leslie had all but vanished since our last meeting, but when she was finally found, she was belligerent and uncooperative. Michael Grant was easy enough to find, but after initially agreeing to be interviewed by *Dateline, 20/20,* and John Walsh, he ultimately declined.

Yet Karen was determined to succeed, so she, too, contacted the prison and attempted to schedule a meeting. Her persistence eventually paid off: Michael Grant not only agreed to an on-camera interview but would also submit a DNA sample despite nearly six years of refusing to do so.

The evening the segment was to air, I was called to the television studio for the results of the DNA test. My own DNA had been collected a few days earlier and was to be compared to the genetic profile of Michael Grant's. Even as Lisa and I drove the expansive concrete riverbeds of highways to our destination, I knew the results would hold no bearing on who I saw when I looked into the mirror. The blood that flowed through my veins was my own—no one else's. The pride or shame I would feel about myself would be of my own doing—the content of my character, not by my genetic makeup.

I parked the car, and we soon found ourselves at a security checkpoint at the lobby's entrance. Once we were cleared, Lisa spotted the reporter waiting by a nearby door to accompany us to the studio. I had grown to understand how the media worked by now, and if DNA results were to be revealed, they wanted it done before a camera.

"Are you a little nervous?" Karen asked as we wove our way through hallways.

"Maybe a little."

I reached a short-backed barstool and took my position across from the reporter as the crew wired me with a microphone.

"As you know," the reporter began, "Michael Grant agreed to submit a sample of his DNA after years of refusal. We asked you to submit your DNA to a local lab for comparison. Mysteries have surrounded you your entire life, including the possibility that he is not your father—that you may have been kidnapped. Well, today I hold the answer to at least part of that mystery."

She produced a white document and held it up for me to view.

"With 99.9% certainty, the lab results of the DNA test revealed that Michael Grant is biologically your father."

"Okay," I breathed with a nod. I remembered times when I would glance quickly in a mirror, and perhaps it was the lighting or the angle, but I could see my father staring back at me. In an expression, or a laugh, there it was; the harder I looked for it, the faster the sensation would fade. Yet now I could look in the mirror, and although I couldn't deny a resemblance, I saw me. I saw Chip St. Clair. Biologically proven or not, I would never again call him "Father," for he had thrown that privilege away. I would never consider that he had given me life, for the life I was leading was of my own design, not his.

"How do you feel?" she probed.

"I'm relieved. Relieved to finally know there is no other family out there suffering with the fear of what might have happened to their child. And relieved to know that at least this mystery is solved. I can close this door . . ."

In the wake of the aired segment, I was inundated by media, hoping to put to rest some of the remaining unsolved mysteries. Through their combined efforts, more doors were closed, while other great, gaping ones were thrust open. I learned conclusively that Leslie was biologically my mother, though not through any effort or admission on her part. Ultimately, the answer rested in letters she had sent me years earlier, which by a stroke of luck I had saved. In DNA testing of the saliva from the stamp she licked and placed on the envelope, it was proven that her DNA matched the profile of a person biologically considered to be my parent. On the other hand, samples from both the locks of hair and the teeth I found in the black trunk were tested and came back inconclusive.

Other curious facts surfaced as well, such as the discovery of a death certificate for John Weaver, Leslie's father. It indicated that he had suffered a heart attack and died in the mid-1960s when Leslie was about sixteen, a blatant contradiction of the story she had told Lisa, describing his brutal suicide when she was only six.

In researching the truth behind my forged birth certificate, one reporter made contact with a woman who had worked for the Elkhart County Health Department in Indiana for nearly thirty years. This was the government agency that stored birth records and birth certificates in the county where I was allegedly born. She very clearly remembered a strange incident that occurred sometime during the mid- to late 1970s. The facility had suffered a break-in, and in examining what was damaged or missing, investigators found that the burglars had stolen not drugs or cash, but a series of blank, pale-green birth certificates, prestamped with a doctor's signature. As many continued to dig, even more demons from the past crept up to the surface from the deep abyss.

Detectives in both Michigan and Indiana uncovered enough evidence to warrant naming Michael Grant as a lead suspect in the brutal murders of five other children—children he may have murdered while on the run. One of the children, the eighteen-month-old by the name of Jeffrey Balsley, died in 1969 under almost the exact same circumstances as the murder of Scott Ingersoll, the crime Michael Grant was convicted of a little over a year later. On a snowy New Year's Eve, Grant was once again babysitting the young boy when detectives believe his fury was unleashed. The autopsy report shows that the child died of a sub-dural hematoma—bleeding in the brain. The county's current forensic pathologist reported that there was no possible way for the child to have caused such a massive internal wound by himself. It had to have been caused by an outside blunt force.

If there is one valuable lesson I learned from Michael Grant, it's that chasing someone else's demons can be elusive, but escaping your own is impossible.

Michael Grant tried for twenty-six years to outrun his own demons, but eventually they found him. They always do.

A blend of murmuring voices filled the gallery of the grand ballroom at the lovely Royal Park Hotel in downtown Rochester, Michigan. Guests sipped champagne and pleasantly mingled around me. I self-consciously adjusted the bow tie of my tuxedo, nodding hellos to familiar faces as they passed, feeling utterly euphoric. Although it certainly felt like one, this was not a dream, but a reality created out of a miraculous opportunity that had come my way only a few months before.

I had taken not just steps along a path opposite my father's, but strides; I was now the founder and regional director of the Michigan chapter of Justice for Children, a nonprofit organization dedicated to advocacy for abused and neglected children. In November 2004, after stumbling across a website for a radio program where I had recently been interviewed, I spotted a logo that would send my life in a completely new direction.

Justice for Children (JFC) was a nationwide, award-winning nonprofit that had been advocating for abused and neglected children for nearly twenty years. The children for whom the organization advocates often fall through the cracks in the system. Founded in Houston, Texas, in 1987 by Randy Burton, a former Harris County prosecutor, Justice for Children has been featured on dozens of national news programs, acclaimed by the American Bar Association, and has received awards from numerous organizations for its tough advocacy on behalf of children who have no other voice in the world.

The phone conversation that took place the following day was one of many that set in motion a strong bond between me and Justice for Children, and I developed the deepest respect for Randy, and the mission the organization relentlessly pursued. I was the living example of the child they hoped to save, and I echoed their passion in my own heart, for I knew what it was to live a nightmare.

They soon asked me to be the founder of the Michigan chapter and expand upon the dream of a better world for our children. I was overwhelmed by the power and the promise of the offer and found myself sobbing in Lisa's arms at the proposal.

*This is it,* I wept. *This is where our journey really begins.*

Within a few weeks, the founder and executive director made the long trip to a wintry Michigan, where we sketched out the blueprints for how the chapter would work. When it came time to create the Michigan JFC Board of Directors, I recruited people within the community I knew to be passionate about issues involving children and dedicated to effecting positive change.

On April 1, 2005, the Michigan chapter of Justice for Children opened its doors with me as the regional director and Lisa at my side as the director of casework. Once stories about our opening hit the papers and the airwaves, we were inundated with calls from people willing to volunteer as advocates, as well as calls regarding advocacy cases, indicating the community's willingness to accept us and the need for our services. Our board of directors grew to include both the Oakland County sheriff and prosecutor, a state senator, and a member of Congress, who had offered assistance in resolving some of my identity theft–related issues.

When we needed to create a slogan, a catchphrase for people to understand at a glance what our purpose was, I submitted a suggestion that is still used to this day:

*In a world where a child's cries echo soft and unheard . . . we hear.*

We were soon up and running at top speed, working on cases and applying for grants. I was invited to speak before community groups, at seminars, and at benefits. In a week's time, I would go from a presentation before the State Bar, to testifying before Michigan's state legislature, to front-and-center in a high school classroom—without a break in between.

And this night I was meeting and greeting guests at our first black-tie fund-raising gala. The evening was a little surreal, and as I joined the crowd for dinner, I marveled at the beauty of the room. Scores of tables draped with fine linens sparkled with elegant place settings and dazzled with colorful floral center-pieces. They were dotted around the room and had been strate-gically placed such that all guests would be able to view the raised stage protruding from the north wall.

To my relief the evening was progressing smoothly, for I had played a major role in planning every detail. Since I knew the order of events and the succession of speakers, I was alarmed when a hush fell over the crowd and an unplanned speaker took the stage. I knew her well; as a staff member for U.S. Congressman Joe Knollenberg, Melissa often represented him when he could not be present in his district.

Once the shock of the disruption wore off, I turned my focus to what she was saying.

"She's speaking about me!" I whispered to Lisa, who also wore an expression of bewilderment.

While holding a framed document in her hand, she began by congratulating the district on the formation of the Michigan chapter of Justice for Children. She briefly described the work that we do to save at-risk children who have been physically abused or neglected.

"Last year," she continued, "Mr. Chip St. Clair called the Justice for Children national office in Houston and said he wanted to make something good arise from his childhood of abuse and violence. Today we honor the Michigan chapter of Justice for Children and Regional Director Chip St. Clair for their dedication to helping abused and neglected children."

I was trembling, my eyes filling with tears. As I stood up, Lisa rose and hugged me tight.

"I love you. I'm so proud of you," she whispered.

"Chip," the speaker announced as I wiped my eyes and joined

her on stage, "may I present to you your Congressional Record."

Applause erupted, drowning out the final syllables, and I held the frame close to my heart while looking out at the audience.

As my eyes adjusted to the stage lights shining from above, I stole a moment to reflect on how I had arrived at this moment. I looked out and found Lisa's eyes filled with pride and great smiles among the guests—friends and family, elected officials, prominent members of the community. I couldn't help but think of the contrast between the moment I found myself cold and alone in the dark, rolling waters of Lake Michigan as a child and this moment, where I now stood surrounded by so many people supporting me, believing in me.

*Because I believed in myself.*

At last I cleared my throat and spoke.

"There is a moment all of us must face. A moment of truth. A moment that defines us, that tests us to see what we are made of. I'd like to share a story with you of such a moment. I was eight years old, and my father had thrown me out of a rowboat into Lake Michigan and rowed away. I remember shivering in the ice-cold water, thinking I was going to die. And then something happened. I can't explain it, but something way deep down in the pit of my soul told me to hang on. We all have that, you know. And while all alone in the water, I remembered a poem I had read called 'Invictus.' It goes like this," and then I recited:

*Out of the night that covers me,*
*Black as the Pit from pole to pole,*
*I thank whatever gods may be*
*For my unconquerable soul.*

*In the fell clutch of circumstance*
*I have not winced nor cried aloud.*
*Under the bludgeonings of chance*
*My head is bloody, but unbowed.*

*Beyond this place of wrath and tears*
*Looms but the horror of the shade,*
*And yet the menace of the years*
*Finds, and shall find me, unafraid.*

*It matters not how strait the gate,*
*How charged with punishments the scroll,*
*I am the master of my fate;*
*I am the captain of my soul.*

The sound of silence was deafening, when finally a single clap broke through, then another, then another, until the entire room was thundering, people rising to their feet.

And as tears fell upon my face, I felt light as a feather, as if I were being lifted high into the air by a gentle breeze. Deep within I knew the time had come for me to soar.

# Epilogue

THE PRESSING OF KEYS reacted in a harmony of chords as Beethoven's *Moonlight Sonata* lifted into the air from the vibration of the sound board. Entranced by the music that came not from the piano, but from deep within me, my fingers danced and fluttered across the keys with grace and tempered patience. The power of the music flowed through me as I played out the first movement's climax and moved into the soft, melancholy ending.

When the final note died in the air, Lisa called to me.

"Chip, that was beautiful."

"I had a good teacher," I said.

"Well, the teacher wants you to know that she is ready to leave anytime you are."

"Let's go!" I said excitedly, leaping from the piano bench.

I hastily bolted into the bedroom to grab my wallet, which I left atop the long dresser. I paused for a moment, flipping it open to examine its contents, when I caught sight of my reflection in the standing mirror fastened to the dresser's back.

My eyes seemed to hold so much more than when I had

drawn my self-portrait years before. The eyes in the portrait reflected sorrow and emptiness, not the light of hope and openness I found in them now.

"Are you coming?" Lisa asked playfully as she peeked in through the bedroom doorway.

"Yeah, I'm coming. But first come here a minute." She did.

"There. Now my reflection is complete," I stated, studying Lisa poised beside me. "When I look at myself, I also see you, because you helped me arrive at who I am today."

We embraced before leaving the looking glass, then left to visit our special place. It was as serene as usual, guests strolling along the winding paths, the droplets of the fountain breaking up the glass on the pond's surface, and the incredible inhabitants who in their silent grace had taught me so much.

We took a favored seat on the short, stone wall that formed the perimeter of the pond, full of its shiny wishes, and I smiled when I felt the sun's warmth trickling through the vaulted glass dome above. The trees and plants that surrounded us seemed to stretch out to greet the sun, drinking in its energy, much like the butterflies that sailed from flower to flower to draw in nectar.

Japanese culture holds that a butterfly is the spirit of a loved one, visiting this world in a new form. The ancient Greek word for soul is "psyche," which also means *butterfly*. The more research I did, the more I found that cultures around the globe and across the great expanse of time have revered these colorful winged marvels. It seems that humankind has forever been fascinated by the unique phenomenon of metamorphosis—even drawn to it subconsciously.

We sat in silence while the fragile creatures flitted and glided and bounced on invisible strings, a palette of colors for any artist to envy painted upon their wings.

I thought back to one of the high schools where I had shared my story. A girl had approached me when I finished my presentation and was packing up. She waited for almost everyone to leave the classroom and finally worked up enough courage to ask me a question.

*How do I put my walls down?* she asked teary-eyed.

*You just did,* I smiled.

Through my journey with Lisa, I came to understand that to open up to another, to make yourself vulnerable, is the beginning of introspection, the transformation into a butterfly. To lower your walls is to reveal the rainbow hidden inside, and that is when your true colors begin to shine through.

In my many speaking engagements and wanderings, I've seen people hurting, people with fear as their master. And in Justice for Children I've discovered startling statistics that reinforce my mission and confirm my suspicion. The post-traumatic stress suffered by an abused child is three times greater than that of a war veteran. This is partly because, unlike soldiers, children have no frame of reference to know that the abuse they're suffering is not normal. They don't understand that the world doesn't have to be the way it is in their home, and ultimately all but the glowing embers of hope are dashed.

*Justice may be swiftly dealt by a multitude unjust.*

*Lest man deny his equal to a man, when returned by death to dust.*

I wrote of justice while pondering how some people—people like my father—impose their own sense of wicked justice on others. They treat others in a way they feel is deserved. People who feel they have authority or power over another, and believe they're justified in behaving any way they see fit, seem to forget that they, too, are subject to justice, and that all of us are equal when returned by death to dust.

True justice must be objective, for it is the tool of both the blessed and the damned, not a means of defining them.

Those titles, I found, we earn ourselves.

When we allow our experiences to define our boundaries, we arrest our character and relinquish our fortitude. We master nothing, not even the hell we begin to reproduce. We all have but one opportunity on this earth. Why can't we take the tools we are given and make this world beautiful?

Butterflies represent the possibility of change, of something once self-serving becoming free and enhancing the world with beauty and purpose. With each passing day I became more convinced that if people could hear my story, could learn what I had endured, and could realize my commitment to walk a path opposite my father's, they may well be inspired to make their own change as well.

I thought back to the volumes of books I read—words that will live in my mind forever—words that changed the world.

*To impact the life of even one person as my life was impacted would provide validation to all I've been through,* I thought.

The world may not have as many butterflies as it needs, but now that I have found my purpose in life, now that I have mastered my fate—there will be one more.

*We must be the change we wish
to see in the world.*

—M. K. Gandhi

# Helpful Resources

**The St. Clair Butterfly Foundation**

Founded by Chip and Lisa St. Clair, and based on principles examined in *The Butterfly Garden*, the St. Clair Butterfly Foundation's mission is to inspire C.H.A.N.G.E.: Creating Harmony And Nurturing Growth Everywhere.

Through creative-arts programs, legislative initiatives, community education and outreach programs, and scholarship opportunities, the Foundation works diligently toward the ideal of making the world a safer and more beautiful place for our children—and helps them to realize their potential to soar. For more information contact:

**St. Clair Butterfly Foundation, P.O. Box 210643, Auburn Hills, MI 48321, www.StClairButterflyFoundation.org**

**Jessica Marie Lunsford Foundation**

The Jessica Marie Lunsford Foundation was established to help children in crisis after the horrific kidnapping and subsequent murder of nine-year-old Jessica by a repeat offender. The Jessica Marie Lunsford

239

Foundation is a result of her father's struggle with the evil that claimed his daughter's life. While we cannot rid the world of this evil, we can contain it so that our children can be free. The Foundation's mission is to fight for tougher legislation against child predators; provide a grassroots awareness and continuous support base; and to search, locate, and help law enforcement apprehend absconder pedophiles. Due to the Foundation's efforts, thirty-three states have enacted some form of "Jessie's Law." For more information contact:

**www.jessicamarielundsfordfoundation.com**

### Justice for Children

Justice for Children (JFC) is a nationally acclaimed, award-winning 501 (c)(3) nonprofit, dedicated to the advocacy of abused and neglected children. Created in Houston, Texas, by former Harris County Prosecutor Randy Harris, JFC has been a leader in identifying and advocating for children who fall through the cracks in the criminal justice system. With chapters in Texas, Arizona, Washington, D.C., and Michigan, JFC utilizes community outreach, educational programs, and legal-aid programs to protect children and keep child predators behind bars. For more information contact:

**www.justiceforchildren.org**

### KlassKids Foundation

In the aftermath of the October 1, 1993, kidnap and murder of his twelve-year-old daughter Polly, Marc Klaas gave up his lucrative rental car franchise to dedicate his life to preventing future tragedies. In September 1994, Mr. Klaas founded the Sausalito, California-based non-profit KlaasKids Foundation with the singular mission of stopping crimes against children. "Polly gave meaning to her life, but I am the one who will give meaning to her death," explains Klaas. "Through the KlaasKids Foundation we can create her legacy and ensure that her death was not in vain."

Through federal and state legislative efforts, Mr. Klaas and the KlaasKids Foundation have promoted prevention programs for at-risk youth, stronger sentencing for violent criminals, and governmental accountability and responsibility. Oftentimes this advocacy takes the form of congressional or other legislative testimony. For more information contact:

**www.klaaskids.org**

## PROTECT

PROTECT is a national *pro-child, anti-crime* membership association founded on the belief that our first and most sacred obligation as parents, citizens, and members of the human species is the protection of children from harm. PROTECT is committed to building a powerful, nonpartisan force for the protection of children from abuse, exploitation, and neglect. For more information contact:

**www.protect.org**

### The Bay Harbor Foundation

The Bay Harbor Foundation was established in 2004 as a charitable, nonprofit membership to support the arts, education, environment and health and human services throughout Northern Lower

Michigan. For more information contact:

**www.BayHarborFoundation.org**

## ChildTrauma Academy

The ChildTrauma Academy, a not-for-profit organization based in Houston, Texas, is a unique collaborative of individuals and organizations working to improve the lives of high-risk children through direct service, research, and education. For more information contact:

**www.childtrauma.org**

# Discussion
# Topics

1. The author wrote each chapter as both a self-contained unit and yet a continuous part of the book as a whole. Discuss the title of each chapter and its significance in terms of the author's life at that moment. What title would you give the current chapter in your life?

2. What is your definition of *justice*? Does the author believe justice is served in *The Butterfly Garden*? Do you?

3. At which point in *The Butterfly Garden* does the author eventually lose hope and begin his descent into despair? Have you ever suffered such a crisis, and how did you get through it?

4. In chapter 6, the author describes daybreak as follows: "Dawn seemed to be so mystical; the few moments before the world awakens, yet still dreams. Dawn was a time when just about anything seemed possible, when something magnificent might happen." Do you find any time of the day or night magical—or menacing? When? Why?

5. The author points out that each of us has a "moment of truth," a moment he experienced in a very literal sense. Compare and contrast his moment of truth, his quest for identity, with your own.

6. In the author's view, "Reality rarely changes; only our perspective of it." Has your view of reality ever changed, prompting you to look at life differently? If so, when?

7. Lisa's love for Chip transcended merely supporting him in his quest; it challenged him to bring out the best she believed to be within. Discuss an example in the book in which Lisa's deep devotion to Chip was apparent. Does someone in your life challenge you to bring out your best?

8. Discuss the significance of the gazebo. Has there ever been a gazebo in your life?

9. Throughout the book, the author describes Leslie's superstitious nature. Do you believe that people with guilty consciences are more superstitious? Is it just a coincidence that Leslie and Michael got caught when they gave up their superstitions?

10. A strong theme in the book is fate versus free will. Do you believe in fate? Do you think events play out as a result of fate, luck, or free will? Explain why.

11. How would you cope with the trials and tribulations described in *The Butterfly Garden* if you were the author? Lisa?

12. "I often think of life as a great darkened room with a mammoth-sized tapestry fastened to a stone wall. All we have is the flicker of a candle's flame to catch glimpses of what the entire picture is to reveal, never quite able to see more than a little at a time. I believe true peace can be achieved not in viewing the whole tapestry, but in accepting without bitterness those portions we

have been afforded the luxury to see. Yet sometimes circumstances arise that shed light on more than expected." This opening of the final chapter describes a sense of reconciliation and peace in accepting situations that defy comprehension. Have events transpired in your life that left you with that empty, resentful feeling of "Why me?" Has hindsight offered any insight? Do you believe that all things—good and bad—happen for a reason?

13. Several places in the book describe the author's reflection in the mirror—at age eight when he tries to look like his dad; as a teenager when he draws a self-portrait with sad, vacant eyes; then at the end when he sees himself and Lisa reflected together. If you had a photograph or a portrait of yourself that shows who you really are, what would it look like and why?

14. What insights have you gained from reading *The Butterfly Garden?* Has it changed your life or your perception of life? If so, how?

15. According to the author, what is the *Butterfly Garden?* Do you have your own butterfly garden?

16. There are several allegorical/metaphorical threads woven throughout *The Butterfly Garden,* such as the author's sinking feeling during his battle with doubt and despair— a strong echo of the incident in Lake Michigan. Have you ever experienced emotional turmoil that resonated with a real-life incident? Is there a metaphor you would use to describe that period in your life?

# Unsolved Mysteries and Unanswered Questions

Many questions and mysteries still loom in the circumstances surrounding *The Butterfly Garden*, questions that may never be answered. As a writer, I was challenged with the monumental task of finding a fitting end in the face of such mysteries; as a person, I know I may never have the answers, and I'm at peace with that. But in my travels and speaking engagements, some common questions always surface, which I've compiled below.

Please visit www.TheButterflyGardenMemoir.com to post your own theories to these and other mysteries, read proposed theories and commentary, and even pose your own questions.

- The author describes a scenario where a mysterious question was posed during an explosive episode by Michael Grant—"Do you want me to tell him what happened when he was three?" Although not included in the book, the author recalls this very question posed several times throughout his childhood. What are possible theories?

- As a child the author saw several scars on Michael Grant,

including a dent in his skull alleged to have happened during combat in Vietnam. When the façade of being a Vietnam veteran was revealed as a lie, a great gaping hole still remained. What was the cause of all the scars on Michael Grant?

• The *Detroit Free Press* reporter examined several peculiar photographs, including one of an infant alleged to be the author in the foreground with a portrait of an older toddler also alleged to be the author hanging on the wall in the background. It is impossible for both children in the photographs to be that of the author. If one is of the author, then who is the other child?

• When the author was around five years old, Michael and Leslie went through the painstaking task of changing and forging new documents from the alias "Carole" to the new alias of "St. Clair." If the alias "Carole" was working fine to conceal their identities, why did they go through all the trouble to change it? Where did the name Carole come from? The name St. Clair?

• After the dark family secret was revealed and Michael Grant was returned to prison, why did both he and Leslie refuse for nearly six years to submit to DNA tests?

• Was it simply a coincidence that Michael Grant murdered Scott Ingersoll on August first, and Chip St. Clair was born on August first, exactly five years later? Or as the author suggests ". . . something far more sinister might have taken place"?

• After Michael Grant's arrest, Leslie made a chilling comment before abruptly ending a phone call with the author, indicating that she had things to burn. Was it evidence of other crimes?

Other things from the black trunk? Also in the book, the author describes a scenario when he met up with Leslie in a park to try to find some answers. If all crimes and mysteries had been revealed, why was she so elusive and paranoid about police wiretaps?

• The author uncovered several mysterious items in the trunk, including locks of hair, Native American jewelry, and a jewelry box full of teeth. Juxtapose this with the moment when the family poodle, Beau, was murdered, and Leslie snipped a lock of hair from the dog before releasing it to the care of the veterinary hospital. What can be inferred by this behavior?

# About the Author

CHIP ST. CLAIR IS the recipient of a U.S. Congressional Record for his ardent advocacy on behalf of abused and neglected children and fights to keep child predators behind bars.

He began sharing his story nationally in 2002, and has been featured on network television programs such as *Dateline* and *Good Morning America*. St. Clair's work often places him in the media spotlight as he fights relentlessly for tough legislation aimed at protecting children, most recently helping to pass Montana's, Maryland's and Michigan's version of Jessica's Law—a law inspired by the kidnapping, rape, and murder of nine-year-old Jessica Marie Lunsford that demands as much a twenty-five-year mandatory minimum sentence for first degree child sexual assault, in addition to GPS tracking devices placed on qualifying child sexual predators upon release.

Today, he shares his inspirational story with children and adults in schools, panel discussions, and seminars, as he lectures both locally and nationally. In his free time he enjoys outdoor activities and indulging in his thirst for great literature. He is currently at work on several new book projects.

St. Clair and his wife live in Michigan with their two Yorkshire terriers, Juliette and Cheyenne.

For more information about Chip St. Clair and his upcoming projects, visit **www.ChipStClair.com**.

**Note to teaching professionals:** Chip speaks to college and high school classes on themes of overcoming adversity, self-discovery through art and literature, and realizing dreams. For information about incorporating *The Butterfly Garden* into class curriculums or lesson plans visit: **TheButterflyGardenMemoir.com**.